Blooms
AND BAKING

Blooms AND BAKING

Add Aromatic, Floral Flavors to Cakes,
Cookies, Candies and More

AMY HO, Founder of Constellation Inspiration

PAGE STREET
PUBLISHING CO.

PAGE STREET
PUBLISHING CO.

First published in 2020 by
Page Street Publishing Co.
27 Congress Street, Suite 105
Salem, MA 01970
www.pagestreetpublishing.com

Distributed by Macmillan, sales in Canada by The Canadian Manda Group.

24   23   22   21   20   1   2   3   4   5

ISBN-13: 978-1-62414-950-4
ISBN-10: 1-62414-950-2

Library of Congress Control Number: 2019942907

Cover and book design by Laura Benton for Page Street Publishing Co.
Photography by Amy Ho
Floral watercolors by Creative Market

Printed and bound in the United States

Dedication

To my parents, for providing the love that allowed me to blossom.

To Rich, for filling my heart with the most beautiful blooms.

Contents

Introduction - 9

    Baking with Flowers - 9

    Floral Syrups - 10

CAKES AND CUPCAKES - 13

Lavender Cake with Creamy Lemon Curd and Vanilla Buttercream - 15

Chamomile Cake with Peach and Mascarpone Buttercream - 17

Elderflower-Strawberry Buttermilk Cake - 21

Chocolate-Lilac Cake with Chocolate Buttercream - 22

Cherry Blossom Almond Layer Cake - 25

Jasmine and Vanilla Bundt Cake - 26

One-Bowl Chocolate Sheet Cake with Buttercream Flowers - 29

Persian Love Cake - 30

"Flowerfetti" Brown Butter Apple Cake with Cream Cheese Buttercream - 33

Woodland Pear Cake with Chestnut and Vanilla Swiss Meringue Buttercream - 35

Chocolate Bundt Cake with Orange Blossom Ganache - 39

White Chocolate Cake with Rose Mascarpone - 40

Lemon-Ricotta Cupcakes with Lemon-Elderflower Buttercream - 43

Lavender "Hot Chocolate" Cupcakes - 46

Lilac-Vanilla Cupcakes - 49

COOKIES - 51

Chewy Lavender-Earl Grey Sugar Cookies - 53

Cherry Blossom Sablés - 54

Floral Almond Wreath Cookies - 57

Dark and White Chocolate-Lavender Cookies - 58

Mixed Berry-Lavender Streusel Bars - 61

Pressed Pansy Sugar Cookies - 62

White Chocolate, Pistachio, and Orange Blossom Cookies - 65

Lavender Caramel and Mocha Thumbprint Cookies - 66

Lavender-Pistachio Linzer Cookies - 69

Rose Petal Shortbread - 70

Plum Blossom "Window" Cookies - 72

CHOUX - 75

Whipped Cherry Blossom Ganache and Matcha Cream Puffs - 77

Chamomile-Mango Cream Puffs - 79

Jasmine-Blueberry Ice Cream Choux Puffs - 83

Coffee and Milk Chocolate Cream Puffs with Candied Rose Petals - 85

Jasmine and Honey Éclairs - 89

Chocolate-Lavender Religieuse - 91

PIES AND TARTS - 95

Strawberry-Rose Pie - 97

Peach Galette with Lavender Whipped Cream - 101

Floral Hand Pies - 103

Pear Pie with Pressed-Flower Crust - 107

Summer Fruit Tart - 111

Strawberry, Rhubarb, and Rose Frangipane Tart - 112

Hibiscus-Glazed Apple-Pistachio Frangipane Tart - 115

No-Bake Honey Blossom Cheesecake Tart with Plums - 118

Apple-Rose Custard Tart - 121

Jasmine Fruit Tartlets - 124

OTHER FLORAL TREATS - 127

Rose Blossom Mochi - 129

No-Churn Rose-Pistachio Ice Cream Sandwiches - 130

Jasmine Mooncakes - 132

Floral Caramels - 135

Rose Lollipops - 136

DECORATION TUTORIALS AND TECHNIQUES - 139

Decorating with Fresh Flowers - 140

Naked Cake Decorating 101 - 142

Making Candied and Pressed Petals for Decoration - 145

Piping Buttercream Flowers - 149

Rose Piping Tutorial - 150

Ranunculus Piping Tutorial - 153

Ruffled Peony Piping Tutorial - 154

Sunflower Piping Tutorial - 157

Chrysanthemum Piping Tutorial - 158

Introduction to Russian Piping Tips - 160

Holiday Floral Cookie Box Tutorial - 163

Acknowledgments - 165

About the Author - 167

Index - 168

Introduction

Falling in love with flowers is one of the quickest ways I fall in love. I love every diaphanous petal but also each imperfection a bloom might carry. Of the many things I wish lasted a while longer, flowers are one of the things I wish lasted forever. And this is why I love baking and decorating with flowers. Putting flowers on a cake makes the blossoms last longer because I get extra keepsakes—the best one being the experience of making and decorating the cake. Adding floral flavors to baked goods means I get to easily share this love of flowers with others too.

In this book, you will find treats that are perfect for baking on a weeknight and eating alongside your morning cup of coffee the next day (if you can wait that long). Some of the baked goods, like the layer cakes, are more of a weekend affair—they might be a bit over the top for everyday purposes, but I wholeheartedly believe that every day is worthy of a celebration with cake.

This book is divided into two main parts: baking with flowers and decorating with flowers. The former is a collection of recipes for cakes, cookies, choux, pies, tarts, and candies. These recipes are little love letters dedicated to all things delicate and sweet. They are inspired by seasonal flavors and florals and by places I have been and flavors that have lingered since. While baking and recipes are grounded in science (delicious science) and a precise understanding of how ingredients work together, decorating is the opposite. Cake decorating, especially with flowers, is my favorite art form. Whether I am decorating with fresh flowers or piping intricate petals, I believe any cake is more beautiful when adorned with flowers. Ultimately, this book is a collection of recipes, stories, and love letters that are sweet to read and even sweeter to eat.

Baking with Flowers

Every flower is beautiful, but not every flower is edible. Many flowers are safe for consumption, but we will be focusing on edible flowers that you can easily find in stores or purchase online. There are multiple ways to add floral flavors to your baked goods: folding the (usually dried) flowers themselves into the batter before baking, incorporating flowers into the filling, turning flowers into floral syrups to infuse into baked goods, and adding flowers directly onto the pastry itself. Including flowers and floral flavors in your baked goods is easy but must be done carefully. Too much and your cake or buttercream can taste soapy or too perfume-like. With buttercreams, ice creams, and other sweets that I do not need to bake, I like to start with a smaller amount of floral flavoring and add more if the flavor is too faint. Tasting as you go is the best bet. This is harder for things like cake batter or cookie dough, but remember that less is always more.

Floral Syrups

A great way to incorporate floral flavors into baked goods, especially cake, is to use floral syrups. Floral syrups are helpful for getting flavors out of certain flowers when baking the flowers directly into the cake or incorporating them into the buttercream is not the best option. It is also a great way to preserve flavors of flowers that are highly seasonal. For example, elderflowers only bloom for a short period during springtime, but when made into a syrup, elderflower flavor can be incorporated in a variety of baked goods throughout the year. Many floral syrups can also be bought in stores. A gentle brushing of floral syrup on a cake layer is an easy and effective way to introduce floral flavor to the finished cake and to keep the cake extra moist. Syrups can also be added to buttercreams.

Floral syrups are extremely simple to make. You only need three ingredients: water, sugar, and the flower of your choice. (Sometimes lemon is added as well.) Generally, the ratio of water to sugar is 1:1—that is, for 1 cup (240 ml) of water, you want 1 cup (200 g) of granulated sugar. With 1 cup (240 ml) of water and 1 cup (200 g) of granulated sugar, I like to add these amounts for each respective flower to make the syrup (add more or less depending on your preference):

- Elderflower: ½ cup (10 g) elderflowers; ½ large lemon, thinly sliced; 1 tablespoon (15 ml) fresh lemon juice

- Lilac: 1 cup (15 g) fresh lilac buds (add ¼ cup [100 g] blueberries for a vibrant purple color)

- Jasmine: ¼ to ⅓ cup (6 to 8 g) dried culinary-grade jasmine flowers

- Chamomile: 3 to 4 bags chamomile tea

- Rose: ½ cup (5 g) dried culinary-grade rose petals

- Lavender: 1 to 2 teaspoons (1 to 2 g) dried culinary-grade lavender

In a small saucepan over medium heat, bring the water and sugar to a boil. Reduce the heat to low and simmer the mixture until the sugar is dissolved, about 3 minutes, stirring at each minute interval. Add the flowers and any add-ins, then simmer the syrup for 10 minutes. Remove the saucepan from the heat and pour the syrup through a filter or fine-mesh sieve into a sealable glass jar to remove the flowers. Let the syrup cool, and then put it in the refrigerator.

The syrups can be refrigerated in a glass jar for up to 1 month. If you need to store a syrup longer, it can also be frozen in an airtight container for up to a year. Note that syrups will not freeze solid due to the high sugar content.

Cakes and Cupcakes

I love flowers. I have always wished that fresh flowers would last longer than their short bloom time. To preserve the beautiful blooms and enjoy them year-round, I incorporate them into cakes and cupcakes. By adding finely ground dried flowers to cake batters and ganache, steeping flowers in milk for cake batter, and turning seasonal wildflowers into homemade floral syrups for buttercream and for brushing on baked cake layers, I am able to appreciate these flowers beyond their bloom time and original form. Fresh elderflower becomes elderflower syrup for Lemon-Ricotta Cupcakes with Lemon-Elderflower Buttercream (page 43). Jasmine flowers are incorporated into cake batter to make Jasmine and Vanilla Bundt Cake (page 26). And fresh lilac from the farmers' market gets transformed into Chocolate-Lilac Cake with Chocolate Buttercream (page 22) and Lilac-Vanilla Cupcakes (page 49).

For additional cake assembly tips beyond the ones provided in each recipe, please refer to pages 142 to 143.

LAVENDER CAKE *with* CREAMY LEMON CURD *and* VANILLA BUTTERCREAM

Lavender and lemon is one of my favorite flavor combinations. Lavender on its own can be an extremely perfume-like and overpowering flavor, but lemon brightens up the cake and cuts through the overly floral notes of lavender. Creamy but not-too-tart lemon curd can be found between each fluffy lavender cake layer, and a classic vanilla buttercream enrobes the entire cake. This creamy lemon curd is handy to have in your refrigerator and makes a great topping for yogurt, ice cream, and other desserts like pavlova!

Yields 1 (6-inch [15-cm]) three-layer cake

Creamy Lemon Curd
1/3 cup (80 ml) fresh lemon juice

2 large eggs

1 large egg yolk

6 tbsp (78 g) granulated sugar

1/4 tsp salt

1/2 cup (113 g) unsalted butter, cubed

Lavender Cake
3 cups (360 g) all-purpose flour

3 tbsp (24 g) cornstarch

1 tbsp (12 g) baking powder

1/2 tsp baking soda

1/2 tsp culinary-grade dried lavender, ground

1/2 tsp salt

1 cup (240 ml) whole milk

2/3 cup (160 g) full-fat sour cream

1 tsp pure vanilla extract

1 cup (227 g) unsalted butter, at room temperature

1¾ cups (350 g) granulated sugar

3 large eggs, at room temperature

2 large egg yolks, at room temperature

Make the creamy lemon curd. Whisk together the lemon juice, eggs, egg yolk, granulated sugar, and salt in a large nonmetal bowl (e.g., glass or porcelain). Place the bowl over a small pot of simmering water, making sure the bottom of the bowl does not touch the water. Heat the mixture, whisking constantly, until it starts to thicken, 5 to 7 minutes. The lemon curd should be thick enough to coat the back of the spoon. Once the lemon curd has thickened, remove the bowl from the double boiler and allow the curd to cool for 10 minutes. Add the butter, one cube at a time, and whisk constantly until all the butter has been combined. Strain the curd through a fine-mesh sieve to remove any clumps. Place a piece of plastic wrap over the curd and transfer the bowl to the refrigerator for at least 3 hours, until the curd is fully chilled.

Make the lavender cake. Preheat the oven to 350°F (177°C). Grease three (6-inch [15-cm]) round cake pans, line them with parchment paper, and set them aside.

In a medium bowl, whisk together the flour, cornstarch, baking powder, baking soda, lavender, and salt. Set the flour mixture aside.

In a medium measuring cup, combine the milk, sour cream, and vanilla. Set the milk mixture aside.

In a stand mixer fitted with a paddle attachment, beat the butter on medium speed until it is creamy, about 1 minute. Add the granulated sugar and beat the ingredients for about 1 minute, until the mixture is fluffy and pale in color. While the mixer is running, add the eggs and egg yolks, one at a time, making sure each egg is incorporated before adding the next. Stop the mixer and add half of the flour mixture and half of the milk mixture. Mix on low until the ingredients are just incorporated. Add the remainder of the flour mixture and the milk mixture and mix until they are just combined with the egg mixture, about 45 seconds.

(Continued)

LAVENDER CAKE WITH CREAMY LEMON CURD AND VANILLA BUTTERCREAM *(Continued)*

Vanilla Buttercream

1½ cups (340 g) unsalted butter, at room temperature

4 to 4½ cups (480 to 540 g) powdered sugar

2 to 4 tbsp (30 to 60 ml) whole milk

2 tsp (10 ml) pure vanilla extract

Flowers of choice, for decorating

Pour the batter into the prepared cake pans. Bake the cakes for 34 to 36 minutes, or until a toothpick inserted into the centers comes out clean. Cool the cakes on a wire rack for about 15 minutes before removing the cakes from their pans to cool completely.

Make the vanilla buttercream. In the bowl of a stand mixer fitted with a paddle attachment, beat the butter on medium-high speed until it is creamy, about 1 minute. With the mixer on low, add the powdered sugar, 1 cup (120 g) at a time. Add the milk and vanilla. Beat the buttercream at high speed until it is fluffy, about 3 minutes. Transfer 1 cup (185 g) of the buttercream to a pastry bag fitted with a large round piping tip.

To assemble the cake, trim off the tops of the cake layers with a serrated knife if the tops are rounded. Place the first layer of the cake on a cake stand or plate. Pipe a ring of vanilla buttercream around the top of the cake layer. Fill the center with some of the chilled lemon curd. Place the second layer of cake on top of the first and repeat this process, topping the second layer of filling with the third cake layer. Frost the top and sides of the cake with the remainder of the buttercream. Decorate with flowers of choice.

CHAMOMILE CAKE *with* PEACH *and* MASCARPONE BUTTERCREAM

I am very thankful that local British Columbia peaches are some of the best peaches one can find. During summertime, I eat at least one peach a day, amazed each time by the flavor and sweetness of the fruit as if it were my first time tasting a peach. In this recipe, sweet, juicy peaches are cooked down and tucked between layers of fluffy chamomile cake. Peaches add a brightness to the earthy floral sweetness of chamomile.

Yields 1 (6-inch [15-cm]) three-layer cake

Chamomile Cake

1¼ cups (300 ml) whole milk

4 bags chamomile tea, divided

2¼ cups (270 g) all-purpose flour

¼ cup (30 g) cornstarch

2 tsp (8 g) baking powder

½ tsp baking soda

1 tsp salt

¾ cup (170 g) unsalted butter, at room temperature

1⅓ cups (265 g) granulated sugar

5 large egg whites, at room temperature

½ cup (120 g) full-fat sour cream, at room temperature

1 tbsp (15 ml) pure vanilla extract

Fresh culinary-grade chamomile flowers, as needed

Flowers of choice, for decorating

Preheat the oven to 350°F (177°C). Grease three (6-inch [15-cm]) round cake pans and line them with parchment paper. Set the cake pans aside.

Make the chamomile cake. In a small saucepan over medium heat, bring the milk to a simmer. Remove the milk from the heat and steep 3 bags of the chamomile tea in the milk for 10 minutes. Remove the tea bags from the milk and allow the milk to return to room temperature. Set the milk aside.

In a large bowl, whisk together the flour, cornstarch, baking powder, baking soda, salt, and the tea leaves of the remaining bag of chamomile tea. Set the flour mixture aside.

In the bowl of a stand mixer fitted with a paddle attachment, beat the butter and granulated sugar on medium speed until the mixture is smooth and fluffy, about 1 minute. While the mixer is running, add the egg whites, one at a time, letting the previous egg white become incorporated before adding the next.

Add half of the flour mixture to the butter-sugar mixture. Add the chamomile milk, sour cream, and vanilla. Mix on low speed until the ingredients are just combined. Add the remainder of the flour mixture and mix until no more streaks of flour remain.

Pour the batter evenly into the prepared cake pans. Bake the cakes for 28 to 30 minutes, or until a toothpick inserted into the centers comes out clean. Remove the cakes from the oven and let them cool completely before frosting.

(Continued)

CHAMOMILE CAKE WITH PEACH AND MASCARPONE BUTTERCREAM *(Continued)*

Peach Filling

1 tbsp (14 g) unsalted butter

3 medium ripe peaches, peeled, pitted, and diced

2 to 3 tbsp (26 to 39 g) granulated sugar (see note)

Juice of ½ large lemon

1 tsp pure vanilla extract

Mascarpone Buttercream

1 cup (227 g) unsalted butter, at room temperature

¾ cup (170 g) mascarpone, at room temperature

4½ to 5½ cups (540 to 660 g) powdered sugar

2 to 3 tbsp (30 to 45 ml) whole milk

1 tbsp (15 ml) pure vanilla extract

Make the peach filling. Melt the butter in a medium saucepan over medium heat. Add the peaches, granulated sugar, lemon juice, and vanilla. Allow the filling to cook, undisturbed, for 2 minutes. Gently cook, stirring occasionally, for 20 to 25 minutes, until the peaches have broken down and the juices have become thick. With a fork, coarsely mash the peaches, leaving some larger pieces intact. Remove the filling from the heat and let it cool.

Make the mascarpone buttercream. In the bowl of a stand mixer fitted with a paddle attachment, beat together the butter and mascarpone on medium speed until the mixture is smooth, about 1 minute. With the mixer running on low speed, slowly add the powdered sugar 1 cup (120 g) at a time. Add the milk and vanilla. Increase the speed to high and beat the mixture until it is smooth and fluffy, about 3 minutes. Transfer 1 cup (185 g) of the buttercream to a pastry bag fitted with a large round piping tip.

To assemble the cake, trim off the tops of the cake layers with a serrated knife if the tops are rounded. Place the first layer of cake on a cake stand or plate. Pipe a thick ring of buttercream around the edges of the cake. Fill the center of the cake layer with ⅓ cup (108 g) of the peach filling. Place the second layer of cake on top of the first and repeat the preceding steps. Place the final cake layer cut side down. Frost the top and sides of the cake with the remainder of the buttercream and decorate the cake with fresh chamomile flowers and other flowers of choice.

Note: The amount of sugar you will need for the peach filling depends on how sweet the peaches are.

ELDERFLOWER-STRAWBERRY BUTTERMILK CAKE

This cake is a great blank canvas for any season—you can easily swap out the strawberries for another type of seasonal fruit, and if you cannot find or make elderflower syrup, any floral substitute would be just as lovely.

Yields 1 (6-inch [15-cm]) three-layer cake

Buttermilk Cake

2²/₃ cups (320 g) all-purpose flour

1½ tsp (6 g) baking powder

3/4 tsp baking soda

1/4 tsp salt

Zest of 1 large lemon

1½ cups (300 g) granulated sugar

3/4 cup (170 g) plus 3 tbsp (42 g) unsalted butter, at room temperature

3 large eggs, at room temperature

1 tbsp (15 ml) pure vanilla extract

1¹/₃ cups (320 ml) buttermilk, divided

1/4 cup (60 ml) elderflower syrup (page 10)

Fresh strawberries, hulled

Culinary-grade elderflower sprigs, for decorating

Lemon Buttercream

1 cup (227 g) unsalted butter, at room temperature

4 to 5 cups (480 to 600 g) powdered sugar

2½ tbsp (38 ml) fresh lemon juice

2 tbsp (30 ml) whole milk

2 tsp (4 g) lemon zest

1/4 tsp salt

Make the buttermilk cake. Preheat the oven to 350°F (177°C). Grease three (6-inch [15-cm]) round cake pans, line with parchment paper, and set them aside.

In a large bowl, whisk together the flour, baking powder, baking soda, and salt. Set the flour mixture aside. In a small bowl, combine the lemon zest and granulated sugar. Use your fingers to rub the lemon zest with the sugar for about 30 seconds, until the sugar is fragrant.

In the bowl of a stand mixer fitted with a paddle attachment, beat together the butter and lemon sugar on medium-high speed until the mixture is pale yellow and fluffy, about 1 minute. Add the eggs, one at a time, adding the next egg only when the previous one has been incorporated. Add the vanilla and mix well.

With the mixer on low, add half of the flour mixture and ²/₃ cup (160 ml) of the buttermilk. Mix lightly before adding the rest of the flour mixture and the remaining buttermilk. Mix until no flour can be seen, about 1 minute.

Divide the batter evenly among the prepared cake pans and bake the cakes for 32 to 35 minutes, or until a toothpick inserted into the centers comes out clean. Let the cake layers cool for 10 minutes in their pans before carefully removing the cakes and transferring them to a wire rack to cool completely.

Make the lemon buttercream. Beat the butter in the bowl of a stand mixer with a paddle attachment on medium speed until it is creamy, about 1 minute. Reduce the mixer's speed to low. Add the powdered sugar, lemon juice, milk, lemon zest, and salt. Increase the speed to high and beat the buttercream for 3 minutes. Add more powdered sugar or milk, 1 tablespoon (8 g or 15 ml) at a time until the desired consistency is reached. Transfer the buttercream to a pastry bag fitted with an open star piping tip.

To assemble the cake, place the first layer of buttermilk cake onto a cake plate or cake stand. Using a pastry brush, apply a generous coating of the elderflower syrup over the top of the cake layer. Add large dollops of the lemon buttercream on top of the cake layer. Place the second cake layer on top of the first and repeat the preceding step. Place the third cake layer on top of the second, then pipe an outer ring of buttercream to act as a "fence" for the strawberries. Garnish the top with the strawberries and elderflower sprigs.

CHOCOLATE-LILAC CAKE *with* CHOCOLATE BUTTERCREAM

When I see lilacs at the farmers' market, I always come home with a basket full of them. Before you even see the stems of lilacs at the market, you can smell their sweet floral and faint citrus notes from a distance. After I return home, these lilacs get transformed into lilac syrup or are perched on top of a cake. Turning lilacs into lilac syrup means I get to enjoy their sweet scent and flavor throughout the year. Lilac is used in this cake two ways: lilac syrup is brushed on the rich chocolate cake layers and lilac flowers are used on the top of the cake as garnish.

Yields 1 (6-inch [15-cm]) three-layer cake

Chocolate Cake

2¼ cups (270 g) all-purpose flour

1¾ cups (350 g) granulated sugar

½ cup (43 g) plus 2 tbsp (10 g) unsweetened cocoa powder

2 tsp (8 g) baking soda

1 tsp baking powder

½ tsp salt

2 large eggs, at room temperature

2 cups (480 ml) cold coffee

½ cup (120 ml) vegetable oil

2 tsp (10 ml) distilled white vinegar or apple cider vinegar

¼ cup (60 ml) lilac syrup (page 10)

Fresh culinary-grade lilac flowers, as needed

Chocolate Buttercream

1 cup (227 g) unsalted butter, at room temperature

3 to 4 cups (360 to 480 g) powdered sugar

¾ cup (65 g) unsweetened cocoa powder

3 tbsp (45 ml) whole milk

2 tsp (10 ml) pure vanilla extract

¼ tsp salt

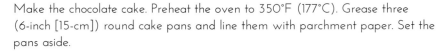

Make the chocolate cake. Preheat the oven to 350°F (177°C). Grease three (6-inch [15-cm]) round cake pans and line them with parchment paper. Set the pans aside.

In a large bowl, combine the flour, granulated sugar, cocoa powder, baking soda, baking powder, and salt. Whisk to combine. Add the eggs, coffee, oil, and vinegar to the flour mixture and mix until incorporated. Scrape down the sides of the bowl with a rubber spatula and make sure there are no dry ingredients at the bottom of the bowl.

Divide the batter evenly among the prepared cake pans and bake the cakes for 28 to 30 minutes, until a toothpick inserted into the centers comes out clean. Allow the cakes to cool in their pans for 15 minutes. Carefully remove the cake layers from the pans and transfer them to a wire rack to cool completely.

Make the chocolate buttercream. In a stand mixer fitted with a paddle attachment, beat the butter on medium speed until it is creamy, about 1 minute. Add the powdered sugar, cocoa powder, milk, vanilla, and salt. Beat the mixture on low speed for 30 seconds, then increase the speed to high and beat the mixture for 2 to 3 minutes. If the buttercream is too thin, add more powdered sugar or cocoa powder 1 tablespoon (8 g) at a time. If the buttercream is too thick, add more milk 1 tablespoon (15 ml) at a time. Transfer the buttercream to a pastry bag fitted with a large round piping tip.

To assemble the cake, place a cake layer on a cake stand or plate. With a pastry brush, brush on a thin layer of the lilac syrup. Pipe tall dollops of the buttercream onto the cake layer until the top of the cake layer is fully covered. Gently place the second cake layer on top of the buttercream and repeat the preceding steps. Place the final cake layer cut side down. With an offset spatula, use the remaining buttercream to cover the top of the cake, creating little "swoops" of buttercream. Garnish the cake with the fresh lilac flowers.

CHERRY BLOSSOM ALMOND LAYER CAKE

When it is cherry blossom season, the only thing I want to do is decorate cakes with their delicate pink blooms. This layer cake uses cherry blossoms both in the cake and on top as decoration. Cherry blossom paste and cream cheese buttercream can be found between three tall layers of fluffy almond cake. Cherry blossom paste or puree can be found at Japanese grocery stores or online. Cherry blossom paste is a mixture of traditional Asian red bean paste (sometimes listed as adzuki bean paste at Japanese stores) and cherry blossom flowers.

Yields 1 (6-inch [15-cm]) three-layer cake

Almond Cake

1 cup (227 g) unsalted butter, at room temperature

2 cups (400 g) granulated sugar

5 large eggs, at room temperature

2½ cups (300 g) all-purpose flour

1 cup (100 g) plus 2 tbsp (12 g) almond flour

1 tbsp (12 g) baking powder

½ tsp salt

¾ cup (180 g) plus 3 tbsp (45 g) full-fat sour cream, at room temperature

¼ cup (60 ml) whole milk, at room temperature

1 tbsp (15 ml) pure vanilla extract

½ cup (120 ml) cherry blossom paste

Fresh or dried culinary-grade cherry blossoms, as needed

Cream Cheese Buttercream

1 cup (224 g) full-fat cream cheese, softened

¾ cup (170 g) unsalted butter, softened

4 to 5 cups (480 to 600 g) powdered sugar

2 to 4 tbsp (30 to 60 ml) whole milk

2 tsp (10 ml) pure vanilla extract

Preheat the oven to 350°F (177°C). Grease three (6-inch [15-cm]) round cake pans and line them with parchment paper. Set aside.

In a stand mixer fitted with a paddle attachment, cream together the butter and granulated sugar until the mixture becomes light and fluffy, about 1 minute. Add the eggs, one at a time, and mix until the ingredients are well combined.

In a medium bowl, whisk together the all-purpose flour, almond flour, baking powder, and salt.

In a large measuring cup, combine the sour cream, milk, and vanilla.

With the mixer running on low speed, add half of the flour mixture and half of the sour cream mixture to the butter-sugar mixture. Mix for 30 seconds. Add the remaining flour mixture and sour cream mixture and mix until the ingredients are combined and no streaks of flour remain.

Transfer the batter to the prepared cake pans and bake the cakes for 33 to 35 minutes, until the tops are golden brown and a toothpick inserted into the centers comes out clean. Allow the cakes to cool in their pans for 15 minutes before carefully removing them to cool completely on a wire rack.

Make the cream cheese buttercream. In the bowl of a stand mixer fitted with a paddle attachment, beat together the cream cheese and butter on medium speed for 1 to 2 minutes, until the mixture is smooth and homogenous. Reduce the speed to low, then add the powdered sugar 1 cup (120 g) at a time. Add the milk and vanilla. Beat the mixture on high until it is fluffy, about 3 minutes.

To assemble the cake, trim off the tops of the cake layers with a serrated knife if they are rounded. Place the first layer of cake on a cake stand or plate. Apply a layer of cherry blossom paste on top of the cake and even it out with a spatula. Apply a layer of cream cheese buttercream on top of the paste. Place the second layer of cake and repeat the preceding steps. Place the final cake layer, cut side down. Frost the top and sides of the cake with the remainder of the buttercream and decorate it with the cherry blossoms.

JASMINE *and* VANILLA BUNDT CAKE

What I love about Bundt cakes is that they are so beautiful without any decorations—the Bundt pan does all the work! It is worth it to invest in a very good nonstick Bundt pan (my favorite is Nordic Ware). A high-quality Bundt pan lasts a long time and almost guarantees that your cake will not get stuck inside the pan, which can be the most devasting thing when you invert the cake. This Bundt cake is very tender due to the addition of cream cheese and sour cream to the batter. It has a dense crumb, and the texture is similar to a pound cake. A light brushing of jasmine syrup adds another layer of flavor to this cake.

Yields 1 (10- to 12-cup [2.4- to 2.8-L]) Bundt cake

2²/₃ cups (320 g) all-purpose flour

¹/₃ cup (40 g) cornstarch

¹/₂ tsp baking powder

¹/₄ tsp salt

1¹/₂ cups (340 g) unsalted butter, at room temperature

1 cup (224 g) full-fat cream cheese, at room temperature

2¹/₃ cups (466 g) granulated sugar

¹/₄ cup (60 g) full-fat sour cream, at room temperature

1 tbsp (15 ml) pure vanilla extract

6 large eggs, at room temperature

¹/₄ cup (60 ml) jasmine syrup (page 10)

Preheat the oven to 325°F (163°C) and generously grease a 10- to 12-cup (2.4- to 2.8-L) Bundt pan with butter or nonstick spray.

In a large bowl, whisk together the flour, cornstarch, baking powder, and salt. Set the flour mixture aside.

In the bowl of a stand mixer fitted with a paddle attachment, beat the butter on high speed until it is smooth and creamy, about 1 minute. Add the cream cheese and beat on high speed until the mixture is completely smooth and homogenous, about 1 minute. Add the sugar and beat on high speed for 1 minute. Add the sour cream and vanilla and beat on high speed until the mixture is combined and creamy, about 30 seconds. Scrape down the sides and along the bottom of the bowl with a rubber spatula.

On low speed, beat in the eggs, one at a time, allowing each to fully incorporate before adding the next.

While the mixer is running on low speed, add the flour mixture. Increase the mixer's speed to medium and beat the batter until everything is just combined and no streaks of flour remain, about 45 seconds. Do not overmix the batter. Scrape down the sides and along the bottom of the bowl with a rubber spatula to make sure all the ingredients have been incorporated. The batter will be thick.

Pour the batter evenly into the prepared Bundt pan. Bang the pan on the counter a few times to remove any air pockets in the batter. Bake the cake for 85 to 95 minutes. Place a sheet of aluminum foil over the cake halfway through the baking time to prevent the top of the cake from overbrowning. Start checking the cake for doneness at the 80-minute mark. The cake is done when a toothpick inserted into the center comes out clean.

Remove the cake from the oven and allow it to cool for 2 hours inside the pan. Remove the cake from the pan by inverting the cake onto a wire rack or serving dish. Allow the cake to cool completely.

With a pastry brush, brush the jasmine syrup over the top and sides of the cake.

ONE-BOWL CHOCOLATE SHEET CAKE *with* BUTTERCREAM FLOWERS

In the past, I was never a firm believer in sheet cakes because I thought they were boring. Why would I want just one layer of cake when I could have two or three? It was not until recently that I realized that a larger single layer cake meant I had more room to decorate. This is my favorite one-bowl cake recipe, which creates an insanely tender and rich chocolate cake. Do not omit the coffee, because it deepens the chocolate flavors. This cake really is a blank canvas—frost it with the back of a spoon, dollop clusters of buttercream using your favorite star tip, or cover the cake with buttercream flowers.

Yields 1 (9 x 9-inch [23 x 23-cm]) cake

One-Bowl Chocolate Cake

1 cup (120 g) all-purpose flour

3/4 cup (150 g) and 2 tbsp (26 g) granulated sugar

1/3 cup (29 g) unsweetened cocoa powder

1 tsp baking soda

1/2 tsp baking powder

1/4 tsp salt

1 large egg

1 cup (240 ml) cold coffee

1/4 cup (60 ml) vegetable oil

1 tsp distilled white vinegar or apple cider vinegar

Vanilla Buttercream

1 1/2 cups (340 g) unsalted butter, at room temperature

4 to 4 1/2 cups (480 to 540 g) powdered sugar

2 to 4 tbsp (30 to 60 ml) whole milk

2 tsp (10 ml) pure vanilla extract

Gel food coloring, as needed

Preheat the oven to 350°F (177°C). Grease a 9 x 9-inch (23 x 23-cm) square cake pan and line it with parchment paper.

Make the one-bowl chocolate cake. In a large bowl, whisk together the flour, granulated sugar, cocoa powder, baking soda, baking powder, and salt. Add the egg, coffee, oil, and vinegar and mix until no streaks of the flour mixture remain. Scrape down the sides and along the bottom of the bowl to make sure no clumps remain. Transfer the batter to the prepared cake pan.

Bake the cake for 26 to 30 minutes, or until a toothpick inserted into the center comes out clean. Allow the cake to cool completely before frosting.

Make the vanilla buttercream. In the bowl of a stand mixer fitted with a paddle attachment, beat the butter on high speed until it is creamy, about 1 minute. With the mixer on low, add the powdered sugar 1 cup (120 g) at a time. Add the milk and vanilla. Increase the speed to high and beat the mixture until it is fluffy, about 3 minutes. Color the buttercream as needed with the gel food coloring. For detailed tutorials on how to pipe specific buttercream flowers, refer to page 150 for roses, page 153 for ranunculus, and page 154 for ruffled peonies.

PERSIAN LOVE CAKE

One of the first recipes I ever shared on my blog was my take on a Persian love cake. A Persian love cake incorporates the flavors of rose, citrus, and pistachios. As its name suggests, this cake is very fragrant and romantic—it's what I would consider a love letter in cake form. Instead of making a three-layer cake like the one on my blog, this cake is a single layer olive oil–based cake that is perfect for every day, because one deserves love letters every day.

Yields 1 (8-inch [20-cm]) cake

1½ cups (180 g) all-purpose white flour

1 cup (200 g) granulated sugar

½ tsp baking soda

¼ tsp baking powder

¼ tsp salt

2 large eggs, at room temperature

¾ cup (180 ml) whole milk, at room temperature

½ cup (120 ml) mild-flavored olive oil

Zest of 1 medium orange

1 cup (240 ml) heavy cream

½ tsp culinary-grade rose water

¼ cup (30 g) salted roasted pistachios, coarsely chopped

Dried culinary-grade rose petals

Fresh figs, halved or quartered

Edible gold leaf

Preheat the oven to 350°F (177°C). Grease an 8-inch (20-cm) round cake pan and line it with parchment paper.

In a large bowl, whisk together the flour, sugar, baking soda, baking powder, and salt. In a medium bowl, whisk together the eggs, milk, oil, and orange zest. Add the egg mixture to the flour mixture in two increments, gently folding the batter after each addition. Fold the batter a few more times until none of the flour mixture is visible.

Transfer the batter to the prepared cake pan. Bake the cake for 40 to 45 minutes, until a toothpick inserted into the center comes out clean. Cool the cake in the pan on a wire rack for 20 minutes before inverting the pan to remove the cake. Allow the cake to cool completely, top side up.

In a large bowl, whisk together the heavy cream and rose water for 2 to 3 minutes, until medium-stiff peaks form.

With an offset spatula, frost the top of the cooled cake with the rose water whipped cream. Decorate the cake with the pistachios, rose petals, figs, and edible gold leaf.

"FLOWERFETTI" BROWN BUTTER APPLE CAKE *with* CREAM CHEESE BUTTERCREAM

Nothing says fall like apple picking. I make this cake and the Hibiscus-Glazed Apple-Pistachio Frangipane Tart (page 115) shortly after I get home from the farm with my bags of freshly picked apples. This cake is the ultimate fall cake—the brown butter adds warm and nutty notes to the apple-studded cake. After frosting the cake with buttercream, edible flowers are pressed onto the sides of the cake to create the "flowerfetti." I love flowerfetti because you can use either fresh or dried edible flowers—making it an accessible decorating technique year-round—and it adds a whimsical floral touch to any cake.

Yields 1 (6-inch [15-cm]) three-layer cake

Brown Butter Apple Cake

1¼ cups (285 g) unsalted butter, divided

2½ cups (300 g) all-purpose flour

1 tbsp (12 g) plus ½ tsp baking powder

1 tsp ground cinnamon

½ tsp baking soda

¼ tsp salt

½ cup (120 ml) whole milk, at room temperature

½ cup (120 g) plain Greek yogurt, at room temperature

1 tsp pure vanilla extract

1¼ cups (250 g) granulated sugar

4 large eggs, at room temperature

2 medium Honeycrisp apples or baking apples of choice, peeled and diced

Edible flowers, as needed

Make the brown butter apple cake. Melt ¾ cup (170 g) of the butter in a small saucepan over medium heat. Use a pan with a light-colored bottom so you can keep track of the butter's color. Swirl the saucepan occasionally to make sure the butter is cooking evenly. After 5 minutes, it will begin to foam. As the butter browns, dark golden flecks (browned milk solids) will appear in the melted butter and produce a nutty and toasty smell. Once all the flecks are brown, pour the butter into a medium bowl, being sure to scrape every bit of brown butter from the saucepan. (If you were to leave the butter in the saucepan, the residual heat would burn it.) Allow the brown butter to come back to room temperature before making the cake batter. You can speed up this process by putting the butter in the refrigerator.

Preheat the oven to 350°F (177°C). Grease three (6-inch [15-cm]) round cake pans and line them with parchment paper.

In a medium bowl, whisk together the flour, baking powder, cinnamon, baking soda, and salt. Set the flour mixture aside.

In a large measuring cup, whisk together the milk, yogurt, and vanilla. Set the milk mixture aside.

In the large bowl of a stand mixer fitted with a paddle attachment, beat together the brown butter, remaining ½ cup (113 g) of butter, and granulated sugar on medium speed until the mixture is fluffy, about 1 minute. Reduce the speed to low and add the eggs, one at a time, until they are well incorporated. Add half of the flour mixture and half of the milk mixture and gently mix to combine them. Add the remaining flour mixture and milk mixture and mix until they are just combined. With a rubber spatula, fold in the apples.

(Continued)

"FLOWERFETTI" BROWN BUTTER APPLE CAKE WITH CREAM CHEESE BUTTERCREAM
(Continued)

Cream Cheese Buttercream

1 cup (224 g) full-fat cream cheese, at room temperature

¾ cup (170 g) unsalted butter, at room temperature

4 to 5 cups (480 to 600 g) powdered sugar

2 to 4 tbsp (30 to 60 ml) whole milk

2 tsp (10 ml) pure vanilla extract

Evenly divide the batter among the prepared cake pans and bake the cakes for 30 to 33 minutes, until a toothpick inserted into the centers comes out clean. Let the cakes cool in their pans for 15 minutes, then remove them from the pans and transfer them to a wire rack to cool completely.

Make the cream cheese buttercream. In the bowl of a stand mixer fitted with a paddle attachment, beat together the cream cheese and butter on medium speed until the mixture is smooth and homogenous, 1 to 2 minutes. Reduce the speed to low and add the powdered sugar, 1 cup (120 g) at a time. Add the milk and vanilla. Beat the buttercream on high until it is fluffy, about 3 minutes.

To assemble the cake, trim off the tops of the cake layers with a serrated knife if the tops are rounded. Place the first layer of cake on a cake stand or plate. Apply the cream cheese buttercream on top of the cake and even it out with a spatula. Place the second layer of cake on top of the first and repeat the preceding steps. Place the final cake layer, cut side down. Frost the top and sides of the cake with the remainder of the buttercream. Gently press on the edible flowers.

WOODLAND PEAR CAKE *with* CHESTNUT *and* VANILLA SWISS MERINGUE BUTTERCREAM

This is decorating inspiration whenever you want to add a winter floral touch to any cake—roses, winter greens, and the cutest miniature gingerbread house. I love to make this cake in the fall and winter months. This cake also combines a few of my favorite wintry things—brown butter, pears, and chestnuts. A brown butter cake studded with pears is filled with a chestnut cream and enrobed in a velvety vanilla Swiss meringue buttercream.

Yields 1 (6-inch [15-cm]) three-layer cake

Pear Cake

3/4 cup (170 g) unsalted butter, at room temperature

1 3/4 cups (210 g) all-purpose flour

2 tbsp (16 g) cornstarch

2 tsp (8 g) baking powder

1/2 tsp baking soda

1/4 tsp salt

1 1/3 cups (266 g) granulated sugar

1 tbsp (15 ml) pure vanilla extract

2 large eggs, at room temperature

2 large egg yolks, at room temperature

2/3 cup (160 ml) whole milk

1/3 cup (80 g) full-fat sour cream

2 small Bosc or Anjou pears, peeled and diced

3/4 cup (175 g) store-bought or homemade chestnut puree

Fresh roses, fresh winter greens, and seasonal figurines, for decorating

Edible gold leaf, as needed

Luster dust, as needed

Make the pear cake. Melt the butter in a small saucepan over medium heat. Use a pan with a light-colored bottom so you can keep track of the butter's color. Swirl the saucepan occasionally to make sure the butter is cooking evenly. After 5 minutes, the butter will begin to foam. As the butter browns, dark golden flecks (browned milk solids) will appear in the melted butter and produce a nutty and toasty smell. Once all the flecks are brown, pour the butter into a medium bowl, being sure to scrape every bit of brown butter from the saucepan. (If you were to leave the butter in the saucepan, the residual heat would burn it.) Allow the brown butter to come back to room temperature before making the cake batter. You can speed up this process by putting the butter in the refrigerator.

Preheat the oven to 350°F (177°C). Grease three (6-inch [15-cm]) round cake pans and line them with parchment paper. Set aside.

In large bowl, whisk together the flour, cornstarch, baking powder, baking soda, and salt. Set the flour mixture aside.

In the bowl of a stand mixer fitted with a paddle attachment, beat together the cooled brown butter and sugar on medium speed until they are smooth, about 1 minute. While the mixer is running, add the vanilla, eggs, and egg yolks, one at a time.

Reduce the mixer's speed to low. Add half of the flour mixture to the butter mixture. Add the milk and sour cream. Add the remaining flour mixture and mix until the ingredients are just combined. Fold in the pears.

Evenly divide the batter among the prepared cake pans and bake the cakes for 30 to 32 minutes, until a toothpick inserted into the centers comes out clean. Remove the cakes from the oven and allow them to cool in the pans for 10 minutes. Remove the cakes from the pans and transfer them to a wire rack to cool completely.

(Continued)

WOODLAND PEAR CAKE WITH CHESTNUT AND VANILLA SWISS MERINGUE BUTTERCREAM *(Continued)*

Vanilla Swiss Meringue Buttercream

½ cup (120 ml) egg whites

1 cup (200 g) granulated sugar

1½ cups (340 g) unsalted butter, at room temperature, cubed

2 tsp (10 ml) pure vanilla extract

Make the vanilla Swiss meringue buttercream. In a large metal bowl, lightly whisk together the egg whites (make sure they are free of any egg yolk) and sugar until they are combined, about 30 seconds. Set this mixture aside.

To create a double boiler, fill a small pot with a few inches of water and bring it to a simmer over medium heat. Place the bowl with the egg white mixture on top of the pot, making sure the bottom of the bowl is not touching the water in the pot. Heat the egg white mixture, whisking it constantly to prevent the egg whites from cooking. Whisk until the egg white mixture becomes very hot and all the granules of sugar have dissolved, 2 to 3 minutes. Dip a small spoon into the mixture and rub the mixture between your thumb and forefinger. If there is any graininess at all, keep cooking until the sugar has fully dissolved.

Once all the sugar granules have dissolved, pour the mixture into the clean bowl of a stand mixer fitted with a whisk attachment. Whisk the mixture on high speed for 6 to 8 minutes, until meringue forms. The meringue should be at medium-stiff peaks and shiny. Stop the mixer and swap out the whisk for the paddle attachment.

With the mixer on low speed, add the butter, two cubes at a time, making sure each addition of butter has been incorporated before adding more.

Once the butter has been mixed in, add the vanilla. Increase the mixer's speed to medium and mix for 4 to 5 minutes, until the mixture is smooth. The buttercream might look curdled or separated, but keep mixing and it will come together. Transfer 1 cup (185 g) of the buttercream to a pastry bag fitted with a large piping tip.

To assemble the cake, place the first cake layer in the center of a cake stand or plate. Pipe two rings of buttercream around the perimeter of the top of the cake. Fill the center with the chestnut puree. Place the second cake layer on top of the first and repeat the preceding steps. Top the second cake layer with the third. Using an offset spatula or bench scraper, frost the top and sides of the cake. Arrange flowers, winter greens, and figurines on the top of the cake. Finish the cake with the gold leaf and luster dust.

CHOCOLATE BUNDT CAKE *with* ORANGE BLOSSOM GANACHE

Orange blossom water is water distilled from the flowers of orange trees. It is highly fragrant and imparts a flavor reminiscent of orange groves and wildflowers. I love the combination of chocolate and orange blossom. It is a play on the traditional festive combination of chocolate and orange, and the flavor of chocolate is deep enough to hold its own against the floral notes of the orange blossom water. Orange blossom water is deceptively strong, so use with a light hand! You can always add more to the glaze after tasting it first.

Yields 1 (10- to 12-cup [2.4- to 2.8-L]) Bundt cake

Chocolate Bundt Cake

2 cups (240 g) all-purpose flour

1³/4 cups (350 g) granulated sugar

½ cup (43 g) plus 3 tbsp (15 g) unsweetened cocoa powder

1 tsp baking powder

1 tsp baking soda

½ tsp salt

2 large eggs, at room temperature

1 cup (240 ml) buttermilk, at room temperature

½ cup (120 g) full-fat sour cream, at room temperature

⅓ cup (80 ml) vegetable oil

½ tsp pure vanilla extract

Orange Blossom Ganache

⅓ cup (80 ml) heavy cream

1 cup (175 g) coarsely chopped white chocolate

Pinch of salt

¼ tsp culinary-grade orange blossom water

Make the chocolate Bundt cake. Preheat the oven to 350°F (177°C). Generously grease a 10- to 12-cup (2.4- to 2.8-L) Bundt cake pan with oil. Set the cake pan aside.

In a large bowl, whisk together the flour, sugar, cocoa powder, baking powder, baking soda, and salt. Add the eggs, buttermilk, sour cream, oil, and vanilla and whisk until the ingredients are fully incorporated, scraping down the sides of the bowl with a rubber spatula to make sure all the dry ingredients are mixed. Pour the batter into the prepared Bundt pan. Tap the pan on the counter a few times to remove any air bubbles from the batter.

Bake the cake for 45 to 50 minutes, until a toothpick inserted into the center comes out clean. Allow the cake to cool in the pan for 15 minutes before inverting the pan to release the cake onto a wire rack to finish cooling.

Make the orange blossom ganache. In a small pot over medium heat, bring the heavy cream to a simmer. Place the white chocolate in a small bowl and pour the cream over the white chocolate. Allow the mixture to sit for 1 minute. Add the salt. Whisk the mixture until the white chocolate has fully melted. Add the orange blossom water and whisk to combine. Set the ganache aside to cool. The cooled ganache should be thick enough to coat the back of a spoon (if it is too warm, it will be runny and the cake will absorb it).

When the cake and ganache have both cooled, transfer the cake to a plate and drizzle the ganache over the peaks of the cake, letting the ganache run down the sides.

WHITE CHOCOLATE CAKE *with* ROSE MASCARPONE

In this recipe, white chocolate is melted and folded into the cake batter to create a cake that is more deeply flavored than a classic vanilla cake. When paired with a mascarpone buttercream lightly scented with rose water, this cake is the dreamiest holiday layer cake. The crumb of this cake is tender and delicate, so be gentle when trimming and layering this cake. This cake features my go-to way to decorate a wintry floral cake: a mixture of winter greens, dark-colored roses, woodland figures like deer and foxes, and shimmering edible gold leaf and luster dust adorn the top of this cake to make it the centerpiece of any holiday dessert table.

Yields 1 (6-inch [15-cm]) three-layer cake

White Chocolate Cake

2⅓ cups (280 g) all-purpose flour

1¾ tsp (7 g) baking powder

¼ tsp baking soda

¼ tsp salt

⅔ cup (117 g) coarsely chopped white chocolate

⅓ cup (80 ml) boiling water

⅔ cup (150 g) unsalted butter, at room temperature

1 cup (200 g) granulated sugar

4 large egg whites, at room temperature

1 tsp pure vanilla extract

1 cup (240 ml) buttermilk, at room temperature

Fresh roses, fresh winter greens, and seasonal figurines, for decorating

Make the white chocolate cake. Preheat the oven to 350°F (177°C). Grease three (6-inch [15-cm]) round cake pans and line them with parchment paper.

In a large bowl, whisk together the flour, baking powder, baking soda, and salt. Set the flour mixture aside.

Place the white chocolate in a small heatproof bowl. Pour the water over the chocolate and cover the bowl. Allow the mixture to sit for 1 minute, then whisk it until the white chocolate has fully melted. Set the white chocolate aside to cool.

In the bowl of a stand mixer fitted with a paddle attachment, beat together the butter and granulated sugar on medium speed until they are creamy, about 1 minute. While the mixer is running, add the egg whites, one at a time, making sure each egg white has been fully incorporated before adding the next. Add the vanilla.

Reduce the mixer's speed to low. With the mixer running, add half of the flour mixture. Once it is incorporated, pour in the buttermilk. Once the buttermilk is absorbed, add the remaining flour mixture. Add the cooled white chocolate mixture and mix until the last streaks of flour are incorporated. Increase the mixer's speed to medium-low and mix the batter for about 20 seconds, until it is smooth.

Evenly divide the batter among the prepared cake pans and bake the cakes for 27 to 30 minutes, until a toothpick inserted into the centers comes out clean. Remove the cakes from the oven and let them cool in the pans for 10 minutes before removing the cakes and transferring them to a wire rack to cool completely.

(Continued)

WHITE CHOCOLATE CAKE WITH ROSE MASCARPONE
(Continued)

Rose Mascarpone Buttercream

1 cup (227 g) unsalted butter, at room temperature

3/4 cup (170 g) mascarpone, at room temperature

4 1/2 to 5 1/2 cups (540 to 660 g) powdered sugar

2 to 3 tbsp (30 to 45 ml) whole milk

2 tsp (10 ml) pure vanilla extract

1/2 tsp culinary-grade rose water

Make the rose mascarpone buttercream. In the bowl of a stand mixer fitted with a paddle attachment, beat together the butter and mascarpone on high speed until they are smooth, about 1 minute. With the mixer running on low speed, slowly add the powdered sugar, 1 cup (120 g) at a time. Add the milk, vanilla, and rose water. Increase the speed to high and beat the buttercream until it is smooth and fluffy, about 3 minutes.

To assemble the cake, use a serrated knife to trim off the tops of the cake layers if they are rounded. Place the first cake layer on a cake plate or cake stand. Generously apply a layer of buttercream over the cake layer and even it out with an offset spatula. Place the second cake layer and apply the buttercream to the top of it. Place the third cake layer on top of the second, cut side down. With an offset spatula or bench scraper, lightly frost the top and sides of the cake with the remaining buttercream. Decorate the cake with fresh roses, winter greens, and seasonal figurines.

LEMON-RICOTTA CUPCAKES *with* LEMON-ELDERFLOWER BUTTERCREAM

Lemon and ricotta is a beautiful spring combination, and even more so when it is paired with elderflowers. Fresh elderflowers can be hard to come by, but elderflower syrups and cordials can be easily found in specialty grocery stores or baking supply stores. Tender lemon-ricotta cupcakes that are made with a mixture of all-purpose and almond flour are topped with a bright lemon-elderflower buttercream and fresh berries, making the perfect spring indulgence.

Yields 12 to 14 cupcakes

Lemon-Ricotta Cupcakes

Zest of 1 large lemon

1 cup (200 g) granulated sugar

1/2 cup (113 g) unsalted butter, at room temperature

2 large eggs, at room temperature

1 large egg yolk, at room temperature

3/4 cup (90 g) all-purpose flour

1/2 cup (50 g) plus 2 tbsp (12 g) almond flour

1 1/2 tsp (6 g) baking powder

1/4 tsp salt

1/2 cup (125 g) ricotta cheese

1/4 cup (60 ml) plus 2 tbsp (30 ml) fresh lemon juice

2 tsp (10 ml) pure vanilla extract

Fresh strawberries, as needed

Fresh culinary-grade elderflowers, as needed

Make the lemon-ricotta cupcakes. Preheat the oven to 350°F (177°C). Line a muffin pan with cupcake liners.

In a medium bowl, combine the lemon zest and granulated sugar and use your fingers to rub them together for about 30 seconds, until the sugar is fragrant. Set this mixture aside.

In the bowl of a stand mixer fitted with a paddle attachment, beat together the butter and lemon sugar until the mixture becomes light and fluffy, about 1 minute. Add the eggs and egg yolk, one at a time, making sure each previous egg has been fully incorporated before adding the next. Mix until the ingredients are well combined.

In a medium bowl, whisk together the all-purpose flour, almond flour, baking powder, and salt.

In large measuring cup, combine the ricotta cheese, lemon juice, and vanilla. Whisk to combine.

Add half of the flour mixture and half of the ricotta mixture to the butter-sugar mixture. With the mixer on low speed, mix the ingredients until most of the dry ingredients have been incorporated. Add the remaining flour mixture and ricotta mixture and mix until the ingredients are just combined. With a standard ice cream scoop, add the batter to the cupcake liners until they are two-thirds full.

Bake the cupcakes for 20 to 23 minutes, until they are golden and a toothpick inserted into the centers comes out clean. Let the cupcakes cool for 10 minutes in the muffin pan before transferring them to a wire rack to cool completely.

(Continued)

LEMON RICOTTA CUPCAKES WITH LEMON-ELDERFLOWER BUTTERCREAM *(Continued)*

Lemon-Elderflower Buttercream

1 cup (227 g) unsalted butter, at room temperature

3½ to 4½ cups (420 to 540 g) powdered sugar

3 tbsp (45 ml) fresh lemon juice

1 tbsp (15 ml) elderflower syrup (page 10) or store-bought elderflower syrup or cordial

2 tsp (4 g) lemon zest

Pinch of salt

Make the lemon-elderflower buttercream. In the bowl of a stand mixer fitted with a paddle attachment, beat the butter on medium speed until it is creamy, about 1 minute. Reduce the mixer's speed to low and add the powdered sugar, lemon juice, elderflower syrup, lemon zest, and salt. Increase the speed to high and beat the mixture for 3 minutes, until the buttercream is light and fluffy. Transfer the buttercream to a pastry bag fitted with a piping tip.

Pipe a swirl of buttercream onto the cooled cupcakes. Top each cupcake with a strawberry and fresh sprigs of elderflowers.

LAVENDER "HOT CHOCOLATE" CUPCAKES

I love lavender because it is very versatile—from the Lavender Cake with Creamy Lemon Curd and Vanilla Buttercream (page 15) to these Lavender "Hot Chocolate" Cupcakes. In this recipe, fluffy devil's food chocolate cupcakes are topped with a dreamy chocolate lavender buttercream and garnished with a large marshmallow. I highly recommend toasting the marshmallow before putting it on the cupcake—doing so transforms the cupcakes into a s'mores-inspired treat.

Yields 16 cupcakes

Devil's Food Cupcakes

1 1/3 cups (160 g) all-purpose flour

1/2 cup (43 g) unsweetened cocoa powder

1 tsp baking soda

1/2 tsp salt

1/2 cup (113 g) unsalted butter, at room temperature

1 cup (200 g) brown sugar

1 tsp pure vanilla extract

2 large eggs, at room temperature

1 large egg yolk, at room temperature

3/4 cup (180 ml) plus 2 tbsp (30 ml) whole milk

1/3 cup (80 g) full-fat sour cream

16 large marshmallows (toasted if desired)

Chocolate-Lavender Buttercream

9 tbsp (125 g) unsalted butter, at room temperature

3 1/2 to 4 1/2 cups (420 to 540 g) powdered sugar

3/4 cup (65 g) unsweetened cocoa powder

3 to 5 tbsp (45 to 75 ml) whole milk

1 tsp pure vanilla extract

3/4 tsp dried culinary-grade lavender, finely ground

Make the devil's food cupcakes. Preheat the oven to 350°F (177°C). Line a muffin pan with cupcake liners.

In a medium bowl, whisk together the flour, cocoa powder, baking soda, and salt. Set the flour mixture aside.

In the bowl of a stand mixer fitted with a paddle attachment, beat the butter on medium speed until it is smooth and fluffy, about 1 minute. Add the brown sugar and mix until it is incorporated.

Reduce the mixer's speed to low and add the vanilla, eggs, and egg yolk, one at a time, adding the next only when the previous has been incorporated. Mix until the ingredients are combined. Stop the mixer and scrape down the bowl.

In a medium measuring cup, combine the milk and sour cream. Turn on the mixer to low speed and add the flour mixture in two batches, alternating it with the milk mixture. Increase the mixer's speed to medium and mix for no more than 30 seconds after the last streaks of the flour mixture are combined.

Using a standard ice cream scoop, evenly distribute the batter among the cupcake liners. Bake the cupcakes for 15 to 17 minutes, or until a toothpick inserted into the centers comes out clean. Let the cupcakes cool on a wire rack for 10 minutes before removing them from the pan. Let the cupcakes cool completely before frosting them.

Make the chocolate-lavender buttercream. In the bowl of a stand mixer fitted with a paddle attachment, beat the butter on medium speed until it is smooth and creamy, about 1 minute. Reduce the mixer's speed to low and gradually sift in the powdered sugar and cocoa powder, scraping down the sides of the bowl occasionally. Add the milk, vanilla, and lavender. Mix until the ingredients are incorporated. Increase the mixer's speed to medium-high and beat the buttercream for 3 to 5 minutes, until it is light and airy. If needed, add additional powdered sugar or milk until the desired consistency is reached.

Transfer the buttercream to a piping bag fitted with a large star tip. Pipe one thick spiral of buttercream on each cupcake before placing a toasted marshmallow on top.

LILAC-VANILLA CUPCAKES

Since I shared the first iteration of these piped lilac cupcakes on my blog several years ago, it has been one of the most popular recipes. The key to achieving realistic piped lilacs is to use two different colors of buttercream in one piping bag. Using two colors adds depth to the flowers and mimics the look of fresh lilacs. My favorite color combinations to use for the buttercream lilacs are pink and purple and purple and blue.

Yields 12 to 13 cupcakes

Vanilla Cupcakes

¼ cup (57 g) unsalted butter, at room temperature

1 cup (200 g) granulated sugar

2 large eggs, at room temperature

1½ cups (180 g) all-purpose flour

6 tbsp (48 g) cornstarch

1½ tsp (6 g) baking powder

½ tsp baking soda

½ tsp salt

6 tbsp (90 g) full-fat sour cream

4 tbsp (60 ml) vegetable oil

1 tbsp (15 ml) pure vanilla extract

2/3 cup (160 ml) whole milk, at room temperature

Whipped Vanilla Buttercream

1 1/3 cups (300 g) butter

4 to 5 cups (480 to 600 g) powdered sugar

3 to 5 tbsp (45 to 75 ml) whole milk

2 tsp (10 ml) pure vanilla extract

Pink gel food coloring, as needed

Purple gel food coloring, as needed

Make the vanilla cupcakes. Preheat the oven to 350°F (177°C). Line a cupcake pan with cupcake liners.

In the bowl of a stand mixer fitted with a paddle attachment, beat the butter and granulated sugar on medium speed until they are smooth, about 1 minute. Add the eggs and mix until they are incorporated.

In a medium bowl, whisk together the flour, cornstarch, baking powder, baking soda, and salt. Set the flour mixture aside.

In a large measuring cup, combine the sour cream, oil, vanilla, and milk.

Add the flour mixture to the butter mixture. With the mixer running on low speed, slowly add the sour cream mixture. Mix until the ingredients are combined, about 1 minute.

Use a standard ice cream scoop to fill the cupcake liners three-quarters full. Bake the cupcakes for 14 to 16 minutes, until they are golden brown and a toothpick inserted into the centers comes out clean. Allow the cupcakes to cool completely before frosting them, 45 to 60 minutes.

Make the whipped vanilla buttercream. In the bowl of a stand mixer fitted with a paddle attachment, beat the butter on high speed until it is light and fluffy, about 1 minute. Reduce the mixer's speed to low; add the powdered sugar, 1 cup (120 g) at a time, and mix until it is fully incorporated. Add the milk and vanilla. Increase the mixer's speed to high and beat the buttercream for 2 to 3 minutes, until it is light and fluffy. Divide the buttercream evenly between two bowls. Add 2 to 3 drops of the pink food coloring to the first bowl of buttercream and 2 to 3 drops of the purple food coloring to the second bowl of buttercream.

Place a large drop flower tip (e.g., a Wilton #2D) into a piping bag. With a rubber spatula, transfer the pink buttercream to one side of the piping bag and transfer the purple buttercream to the other side; this will allow the buttercream lilacs to have two tones.

Pipe dollops of buttercream lilac flowers on each cupcake until the top of cupcake is covered (page 149).

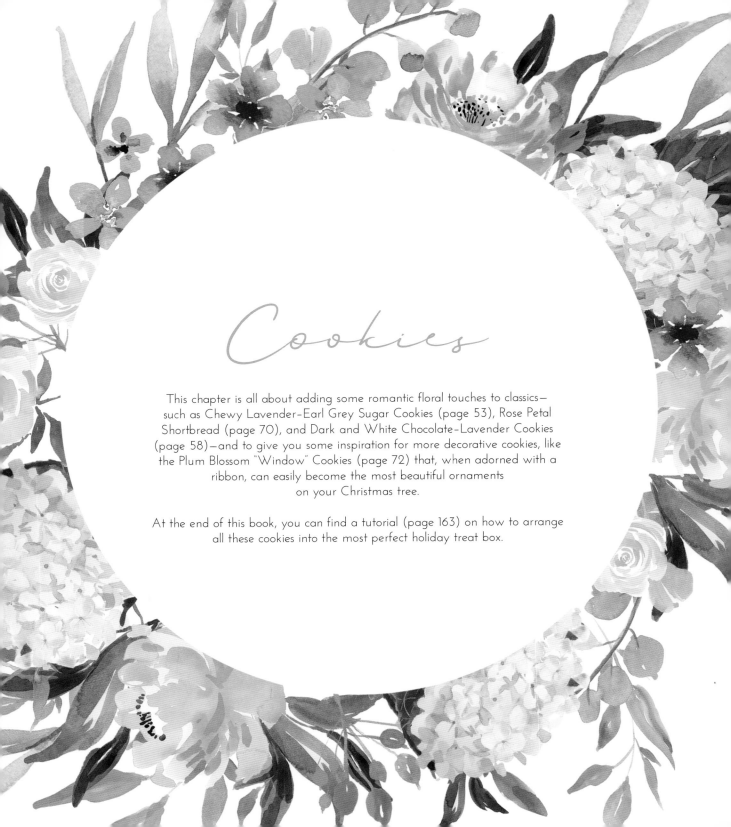

Cookies

This chapter is all about adding some romantic floral touches to classics—such as Chewy Lavender-Earl Grey Sugar Cookies (page 53), Rose Petal Shortbread (page 70), and Dark and White Chocolate-Lavender Cookies (page 58)—and to give you some inspiration for more decorative cookies, like the Plum Blossom "Window" Cookies (page 72) that, when adorned with a ribbon, can easily become the most beautiful ornaments on your Christmas tree.

At the end of this book, you can find a tutorial (page 163) on how to arrange all these cookies into the most perfect holiday treat box.

CHEWY LAVENDER-EARL GREY SUGAR COOKIES

While it may seem intuitive, I learned how sugar affects a cookie's behavior through making many batches of sugar cookies. I am not talking about how less or more sugar influences a cookie's sweetness but how more sugar contributes to the spread and crunch of a cookie. Compared to traditional cutout sugar cookies often used for cookie decorating, these have a crispy golden-brown edge and soft and chewy center. These cookies are scented with both Earl Grey and lavender, a tea and floral combination that I love.

Yields 16 cookies

1 cup (227 g) unsalted butter, at room temperature

1¼ cups (250 g) plus 2 tbsp (26 g) granulated sugar, divided

1 large egg, at room temperature

2 tsp (10 ml) pure vanilla extract

2¼ cups (270 g) all-purpose flour

3 bags Earl Grey tea

½ tsp culinary-grade lavender, finely ground

½ tsp baking powder

¼ tsp baking soda

½ tsp salt

Preheat the oven to 350°F (177°C). Line a large baking sheet with parchment paper. Set the baking sheet aside.

In the bowl of a stand mixer fitted with a paddle attachment, beat together the butter and 1¼ cups (250 g) of the sugar on medium speed until they are smooth, about 30 seconds. Add the egg and vanilla and beat to combine.

In a medium bowl, whisk together the flour, contents of the Earl Grey tea bags, lavender, baking powder, baking soda, and salt.

Add the flour mixture to the butter mixture and mix on low speed until just combined and no more streaks of the flour mixture remain, about 45 seconds.

Using a standard ice cream scoop, portion out dough balls and place them onto a small baking sheet. If at this point the cookie dough is very tacky and soft, cover the dough balls with plastic wrap and chill them in the refrigerator for 20 to 30 minutes. Sprinkle the tops of the dough balls with the remaining 2 tablespoons (26 g) of sugar before baking.

Place 16 balls of dough on the prepared baking sheet, leaving 2 inches (5 cm) between each ball. Bake the cookies for 10 to 13 minutes, until the edges of the cookies are light golden brown. Do not overbake the cookies. Remove the cookies from the oven and allow them to cool on the baking sheet for 10 minutes before transferring them to a wire rack to cool completely.

CHERRY BLOSSOM SABLÉS

These butter cookies are topped with a salty-sweet preserved cherry blossom and are the best way to make the fleeting cherry blossom season last just a bit longer. Preserved cherry blossoms can be found at Japanese markets or online. Because this cookie is such a butter-forward recipe, I like to use the highest-quality butter I can find. I have a "good butter" compartment in my refrigerator filled with blocks of grass-fed, high-fat butter, and I like to use them for this recipe. You will really be able to taste the difference with these cookies.

Yields 22 to 24 cookies

22 to 24 preserved cherry blossoms

2/3 cup (151 g) plus 1 tsp unsalted butter, at room temperature

1/3 cup (67 g) granulated sugar

1½ cups (180 g) all-purpose flour

2 tsp (2 g) cherry blossom powder or few drops pink coloring (optional)

¼ tsp salt

½ cup (100 g) coarse sanding sugar

If the preserved cherry blossoms were preserved in salt, soak them in cold water for 30 minutes. Pat the cherry blossoms dry and set aside.

In a stand mixer fitted with a paddle attachment or in a large bowl with a hand mixer, mix the butter on medium speed until it is smooth and creamy, about 1 minute. Add the granulated sugar and mix until the butter and sugar are smooth, about 1 minute. Scrape down the bowl as needed. With the mixer on low speed, mix in the flour, cherry blossom powder (if using), and salt, just until the ingredients are blended.

Lightly flour a work surface. Transfer the dough to the work surface and knead it gently a few times, until the dough is uniform in texture. Divide the dough in half and shape each half into a 6-inch (15-cm) log. Sprinkle the sanding sugar onto a large baking sheet or rectangular plate and roll the logs in the sanding sugar to coat the sides of each log completely. Wrap the logs in plastic wrap and refrigerate them for at least 1 hour.

Preheat the oven to 325°F (163°C). Line a large baking sheet with parchment paper.

Using a knife, cut the dough logs into ½-inch (13-mm) thick rounds. Put them on the prepared baking sheet, leaving about 2 inches (5 cm) between each cookie. Gently press a preserved cherry blossom onto the top of each cookie.

Bake the cookies for 20 to 22 minutes, or until the edges are golden brown. Let them cool on the baking sheets for 5 minutes before carefully transferring them to a cooling rack. Allow the cookies to cool completely before serving.

FLORAL ALMOND WREATH COOKIES

San Francisco is one of my favorite cities to visit and when I am there, I always make Craftsman and Wolves one of my first stops. The last time I visited Craftsman and Wolves with friends, we ordered seven different pastries to share because everything looked too good not to try. Their shortbread cookies with edible flowers always catch my eye, and I can never leave without buying a few extra to take home with me. This is an ode to one of my favorite bakeries and cities and my perfect holiday cookie.

Yields 18 to 20 cookies

Almond Cookie Wreaths

1/2 cup (113 g) unsalted butter, at room temperature

1/2 cup (60 g) powdered sugar

1/2 tsp pure vanilla extract

3/4 cup (90 g) plus 2 tbsp (12 g) all-purpose flour

1/4 cup (25 g) almond flour

1/2 tsp salt

Fresh or dried edible flowers, as needed (for a tutorial on how to press and dry flowers, go to page 146)

Royal Icing Glaze

1 cup (120 g) powdered sugar

2 to 3 tbsp (30 to 45 ml) whole milk

1/2 tsp rose water

Make the almond cookie wreaths. In the bowl of a stand mixer fitted with a paddle attachment, beat the butter on low speed until it is smooth, about 1 minute. Add the powdered sugar and vanilla and mix until the sugar is fully incorporated and the mixture is creamy. Scrape down the sides of the bowl, then add the all-purpose flour, almond flour, and salt. Mix on low speed for 45 seconds, just until the mixture is uniform in texture.

Gather the dough into a ball, shape it into a disk, and wrap it tightly in plastic wrap. Chill the dough in the refrigerator for at least 60 minutes. Once the dough has chilled, transfer it to a piece of parchment paper, cover it with a second piece of parchment paper, and flatten it with a rolling pin to form a rectangle about 1/4 inch (6 mm) thick.

Preheat the oven to 350°F (177°C). Line a large baking sheet with parchment paper. Using a large and a medium round cookie cutter, stamp out wreaths from the dough. Place the cookies on the prepared baking sheet, spacing them 1 inch (2.5 cm) apart. If at this point the cookie dough has softened, place the baking sheet in the fridge or freezer to allow the cutouts to firm up. This will allow the cookies to retain their shape. Bake the cookies for 10 to 12 minutes, until they are golden around the edges. Let them cool on the baking sheet for at least 10 minutes before transferring them to a wire rack. Let the cookies cool completely before decorating.

Make the royal icing glaze. In a shallow bowl, whisk together the powdered sugar, milk, and rose water. (Add more or less milk to reach the desired consistency.) Dip one side of the cookie wreaths in the glaze and place the cookies on a wire rack to decorate. Immediately place the edible flowers on the cookies before the glaze sets. Allow the glaze to dry completely.

DARK *and* WHITE CHOCOLATE-LAVENDER COOKIES

For me, the holidays are about decorative rolled-out sugar cookies, cutout cookies, bar cookies, and drop cookies. But, of course, we have to have at least one thick and chewy cookie in the mix, and these are the ones: thick cookies boasting puddles of dark and white chocolate with the slight hint of lavender. It is important to use good-quality chocolate here and not waxy chocolate chips. There might be a time and place for chocolate chips, but in order to have puddles of chocolate, you need chunks of good chocolate in the dough. Lastly, I give these cookies a generous sprinkle of flaky sea salt, which, in my opinion, is necessary for any cookie.

Yields 16 cookies

½ cup (113 g) plus 2 tbsp (28 g) unsalted butter, at room temperature

½ cup (100 g) plus 2 tbsp (26 g) brown sugar

½ cup (100 g) granulated sugar

2 tsp (10 ml) pure vanilla extract

1 large egg, at room temperature

1¾ cups (210 g) plus 2 tbsp (10 g) all-purpose flour

1 tsp salt

¾ tsp baking powder

½ tsp baking soda

½ tsp culinary-grade lavender, finely ground

⅔ cup (117 g) coarsely chopped dark chocolate

⅔ cup (117 g) coarsely chopped white chocolate

Maldon sea salt flakes, as needed

In the bowl of a stand mixer fitted with a paddle attachment, cream the butter, brown sugar, and granulated sugar on medium speed until they are smooth, about 1 minute.

Add the vanilla and egg to the butter mixture and mix on medium speed until they are fully incorporated, scraping down the sides of the bowl as needed.

In a medium bowl, whisk together the flour, salt, baking powder, baking soda, and lavender. With the mixer on low speed, add the flour mixture in two batches to the butter mixture, and mix until the ingredients are just combined, about 1 minute.

Add the dark chocolate and white chocolate and mix until they are just incorporated with the dough, about 30 seconds.

Cover the dough with plastic wrap or place it in an airtight container, then refrigerate it for at least 1 hour.

Preheat the oven to 350°F (177°C). Line a large baking sheet with parchment paper.

With a standard ice cream scoop, form balls of dough and place them about 2 inches (5 cm) apart on the baking sheet. Bake the cookies for 12 to 14 minutes, or until the cookies are browned and caramelized along the edges and the centers are just set.

Top each cookie with a sprinkling of the Maldon sea salt flakes. Allow the cookies to cool on the baking sheet for 5 minutes, then transfer them to a wire rack to cool completely.

MIXED BERRY-LAVENDER STREUSEL BARS

I had my first bake sale a few years ago when a local coffee shop was nice enough to ask me to do a small pop-up at their café during the holidays. The strawberry streusel bar was the most popular, and since then, I have enjoyed creating seasonal versions of the bar for friends and family: the classic strawberry version for summer, a blueberry version for the end of summer, and a cranberry one for the holidays. This particular streusel bar is great with whatever berries are in season—or you can use a mix, like I have in this recipe. Instead of using a cinnamon streusel for these bars, I sprinkle them with a lavender-oat streusel before baking, which is a nice contrast against the tanginess of the berry filling.

Yields 9 large bars

Crust
1 cup (227 g) unsalted butter, at room temperature

1/3 cup (67 g) granulated sugar

2 tsp (10 ml) pure vanilla extract

1/2 tsp salt

2 cups (240 g) all-purpose flour

Filling
1¼ cups (300 g) berry jam or preserves of choice

1/2 cup (72 g) fresh blackberries

1/2 cup (72 g) fresh strawberries, hulled and quartered

Lavender-Oat Streusel
3 tbsp (15 g) old-fashioned oats

1/4 cup (50 g) brown sugar

1/2 tsp culinary-grade lavender, finely ground

5 tbsp (25 g) all-purpose flour

1/4 cup (57 g) plus 1 tbsp (14 g) cold unsalted butter, cubed

Preheat the oven to 350°F (177°C). Line the bottom and sides of an 9 x 9-inch (23 x 23-cm) square baking pan with parchment paper, leaving about 1 inch (2.5 cm) of overhang on the sides to serve as handles. Set the baking pan aside.

Make the crust. In the bowl of a stand mixer fitted with a paddle attachment, combine the butter, granulated sugar, vanilla, and salt. Mix on medium speed until the ingredients are combined, about 30 seconds. Add the flour, reduce the mixer's speed to low, and mix until everything is combined, about 1 minute. Press the mixture evenly into the prepared baking pan. Bake the crust for 15 minutes, until it is light golden brown.

Make the filling. Spread the jam over the warm crust. Top the jam with the blackberries and strawberries.

Make the lavender-oat streusel. In a medium bowl, whisk together the oats, brown sugar, lavender, and flour. Cut in the butter with a pastry cutter or a fork until the mixture becomes coarse, pea-size crumbs. Some larger crumbs are okay. Sprinkle the streusel over the filling and bake the bar square for 35 to 40 minutes, or until the streusel is golden brown and the filling is bubbling around the edges.

Remove the baking pan from the oven and allow the bar square to cool for at least 1 hour (preferably until it is completely cool). If you try to lift the bar square out of the pan when it is still hot, the crust can break in half very easily. Lift the bar square out of the baking pan using the parchment overhang on the sides. Cut the square into bars with a large knife.

PRESSED PANSY SUGAR COOKIES

This is the sugar cookie recipe I make every holiday; it was originally shared with me by my aunt Yunche. It is my go-to recipe when I need a perfectly tender vanilla cookie for decorating with royal icing. This holiday season, I am trading in my royal icing for some edible flowers to make these pressed pansy sugar cookies. Topping each cookie with sparkling sugar adds a festive touch.

Yields 24 cookies

1⅓ cups (300 g) unsalted butter, at room temperature

½ cup (100 g) granulated sugar, plus more as needed

2 large egg yolks

1 tsp pure vanilla

2½ cups (300 g) all-purpose flour

½ tsp salt

1 large egg white

24 edible pansies

In the bowl of a stand mixer fitted with a paddle attachment, beat together the butter and sugar on medium speed until they are smooth, about 1 minute. Beat in the egg yolks, one at a time. Add the vanilla and beat until it is fully combined.

Reduce the mixer's speed to low and add the flour and salt. Mix until they are just incorporated, about 45 seconds. Do not overmix. Remove the dough from the stand mixer bowl. Tightly wrap the dough in plastic wrap and transfer it to the refrigerator to chill until it is no longer sticky to the touch, about 1 hour.

Preheat the oven to 315°F (157°C). Line a large baking sheet with parchment paper.

Roll out the dough between 2 sheets of parchment paper until it is ¼ inch (6 mm) thick. Use cookie cutters to cut the dough into your desired shapes. Transfer the cookies to the prepared baking sheet, leaving about 1 inch (2.5 cm) of space between each cookie.

In a small bowl, whisk the egg white to loosen it. Set it aside.

Bake the cookies for 12 to 14 minutes, just until the edges are golden brown. At the 7-minute mark, remove the cookies from the oven and use a pastry brush to brush a very thin layer of the egg white on the top of each cookie. Gently place an edible pansy on top of each cookie and brush a second thin layer of egg wash on top. Sprinkle each cookie with additional sugar and return the cookies to the oven to bake until their edges are golden brown.

Let the cookies cool on the baking sheet for 10 minutes before transferring them to a wire rack to cool completely.

WHITE CHOCOLATE, PISTACHIO, *and* ORANGE BLOSSOM COOKIES

In this recipe, crisp and buttery brown sugar cookies with a hint of orange blossom are studded with white chocolate and pistachios for the perfect cookie to accompany a cup of tea. The dough for these slice-and-bake cookies can be made in advance, kept in the freezer, and baked when you need cookies in a pinch.

Yields 32 cookies

3/4 cup (170 g) unsalted butter, at room temperature

1/3 cup (67 g) packed dark brown sugar

1/3 cup (67 g) granulated sugar

1 large egg, at room temperature

1 tsp pure vanilla extract

1/2 tsp culinary-grade orange blossom water

2 cups (240 g) all-purpose flour

1/2 tsp salt

3/4 cup (130 g) coarsely chopped white chocolate

2/3 cup (80 g) salted roasted pistachios, coarsely chopped

Coarse sanding sugar, as needed

In the bowl of a stand mixer fitted with a paddle attachment, beat together the butter, brown sugar, and granulated sugar on medium speed until they are creamy, about 1 minute. Beat in the egg, vanilla, and orange blossom water. Reduce the mixer's speed to low and beat in the flour and salt until they are just combined. With the mixer still on low speed, add the white chocolate and pistachios and mix until the ingredients are combined.

Dust a work surface with flour. Transfer the dough to the work surface and divide it in two. Shape each half into an 8-inch (20-cm) log. Roll each log in the coarse sanding sugar. Tightly wrap the logs in plastic wrap and chill them in the refrigerator for at least 1 hour (preferably overnight).

Preheat the oven to 350°F (177°C). Line a large baking sheet with parchment paper.

Slice each dough log into 16 cookies just under 1/2 inch (13 mm) thick and place the cookies on the prepared baking sheet about 2 inches (5 cm) apart. Bake the cookies for 12 to 14 minutes, or until they are deep golden brown around the edges. Remove the cookies from the oven and allow them to cool on the baking sheet for 10 minutes before transferring them to a wire rack to cool completely.

LAVENDER CARAMEL *and* MOCHA THUMBPRINT COOKIES

This is an extremely chocolaty cookie that is both crispy and chewy. A creamy lavender caramel fills the center of each cookie, making it the perfect two-bite cookie. If you do not have a thumbprint cookie stamp, you can make these using a traditional thumbprint cookie method. It will be just as good, I promise.

Yields 24 cookies

Mocha Cookies

1 cup (120 g) all-purpose flour

1/2 cup (43 g) unsweetened cocoa powder

1/4 tsp espresso powder

1/4 tsp salt

1/2 cup (113 g) unsalted butter, at room temperature

2/3 cup (133 g) granulated sugar

1 large egg yolk

1 tsp pure vanilla extract

Lavender Caramel

1 cup (200 g) granulated sugar

6 tbsp (84 g) unsalted butter, cubed

1/2 cup (120 ml) heavy cream

1/2 tsp pure vanilla extract

1/2 tsp culinary-grade lavender, finely ground

1/4 tsp salt

Make the mocha cookies. Preheat the oven to 350°F (177°C). Line a large baking sheet with parchment paper.

In a medium bowl, whisk together the flour, cocoa powder, espresso powder, and salt. In the bowl of a stand mixer fitted with a paddle attachment, beat the butter and sugar on medium speed until they are creamy, about 1 minute. Reduce the mixer's speed to low and add the egg yolk and vanilla. Gradually beat in the flour mixture and mix until just combined, about 1 minute. Cover the cookie dough with plastic wrap and chill it in the refrigerator for 1 hour.

Divide the dough into 24 pieces and roll them into balls. Using a thumbprint cookie stamp or your thumb, gently press an indentation into the center of each cookie. Place each cookie 1 inch (2.5 cm) apart on the prepared baking sheet. Bake the cookies for 12 to 14 minutes, until they are just set. They will firm up as they cool. Allow the cookies to cool on the baking sheet for 10 minutes before transferring them to a wire rack to cool completely.

Make the lavender caramel. Put the sugar in a medium pot and spread it over the bottom of the pot evenly. Heat the sugar over medium-high heat, stirring constantly with a wooden spoon. The sugar will form clumps, but after about 6 minutes, it will melt and turn into a dark amber-colored liquid. As soon as the sugar is liquefied, reduce the heat to medium-low. Add the butter and stir until it is incorporated. While stirring constantly, drizzle in the heavy cream and vanilla. Boil the mixture for 1 minute, stirring constantly, then remove the pot from the heat and stir in the lavender and salt. Transfer the caramel to a medium bowl and let it cool completely.

To assemble the cookies, spoon about 1/4 teaspoon of the lavender caramel into the indentation of each cookie.

Note: You will have leftover caramel, but do not be tempted to divide the recipe in half. Making a very small batch of caramel means it can burn much more easily during the cooking process. Any leftover caramel is great on ice cream!

LAVENDER-PISTACHIO LINZER COOKIES

Pistachios are my favorite nut to use in baking. Besides imparting the most beautiful green color, pistachios add a unique sweetness and toasty flavor to any cookie or cake. These pistachio butter cookies are great on their own, but they're even better when paired with a dreamy lavender–white chocolate ganache.

Yields 18 to 20 sandwich cookies

Pistachio Butter Cookies

1¼ cup (150 g) all-purpose flour

½ cup (50 g) pistachio meal

½ tsp salt

½ cup (113 g) unsalted butter, at room temperature

⅓ cup (67 g) granulated sugar

1 large egg yolk, at room temperature

1 tsp vanilla extract

Powdered sugar, as needed

Lavender–White Chocolate Ganache

⅔ cup (117 g) white chocolate, finely chopped

½ cup (120 ml) heavy cream

½ tsp culinary-grade lavender, finely ground

Make the pistachio butter cookies. Preheat the oven to 350°F (177°C). Line a large baking sheet with parchment paper.

In a medium bowl, whisk together the flour, pistachio meal, and salt. Set the flour mixture aside. In the bowl of a stand mixer fitted with a paddle attachment, beat together the butter and granulated sugar on medium speed until the butter is creamy, about 30 seconds. Beat in the egg yolk and vanilla and mix until they are well combined. With the mixer running on low speed, add the flour mixture to the butter mixture and mix until the ingredients are incorporated and the dough comes together as a ball, about 45 seconds. Shape the dough into a disk, tightly wrap it in plastic wrap, and chill it in the refrigerator for 30 to 60 minutes.

Lightly flour a work surface. With a rolling pin, roll out the chilled dough until it is ⅛ inch (3 mm) thick. Using your favorite cookie cutter, cut out the cookies. For every cookie you cut out, you will need to cut out an identical cookie, which will be the top cookie in the sandwich and have a cutout in the center. Place the cookies on the prepared baking sheet, leaving 1 inch (2.5 cm) between each cookie. Once the cookie cutouts have been transferred to the baking sheet, use a smaller cookie cutter and cut out the centers of half of the cookies

Bake the cookies for 6 to 8 minutes, or until the bottoms are golden. Remove the baking sheet from the oven. Cool the cookies on the baking sheet for 10 minutes, then transfer them to a wire rack. Allow the cookies to cool completely before adding the lavender–white chocolate ganache to the centers.

Make the lavender–white chocolate ganache. Place the white chocolate in a medium heatproof bowl. In a small saucepan over medium heat, heat the heavy cream for 2 to 3 minutes, until it starts to lightly simmer. Remove the cream from the heat and pour it on top of the white chocolate. Let the chocolate and cream sit for 2 to 3 minutes. Whisk the mixture until the white chocolate has fully melted. Whisk in the lavender.

Allow the ganache to cool for at least 30 minutes before using. If the ganache is still a bit runny, place it in the refrigerator for 15 minutes before filling the cookies. Dust all of the cookies with cutouts with the powdered sugar. Using a spoon, fill the bottom cookies with a large dollop of the ganache and place the top cookies on the ganache immediately.

ROSE PETAL SHORTBREAD

When I was growing up, my most favorite treat to share with my mom was Walkers brand Scottish shortbread fingers. She always kept a box in her bedside drawer that she would take out whenever we were watching television in her room. The cookies were deliciously buttery, but my favorite part about those cookies was the light dusting of sugar on top. These rose petal shortbread cookies are the grown-up version of the ones I indulged in as a child. They are extremely buttery—I always save my highest-quality butter for these—and are topped with sugar and crushed rose petals.

Yields 1 (9 x 5-inch [23 x 13-cm]) loaf pan

¾ cup (90 g) plus 3 tbsp (15 g) all-purpose flour

¼ cup (30 g) cornstarch

¼ tsp salt

½ cup (113 g) plus 1 tbsp (14 g) very soft unsalted butter

5 tbsp (65 g) granulated sugar, divided

Crushed culinary-grade dried rose petals, as needed

Preheat the oven to 325°F (163°C). Butter a 9 x 5-inch (23 x 13-cm)loaf pan and line it with parchment paper.

In a medium bowl, whisk together the flour, cornstarch, and salt. Set the flour mixture aside.

In the bowl of a stand mixer fitted with a paddle attachment, beat the butter and 3 tablespoons (39 g) of the sugar on medium speed until they are creamy, about 30 seconds. Add the flour mixture. Reduce the mixer's speed to low and mix until a smooth dough forms, about 1 minute. Pat the dough evenly into the prepared loaf pan. Bake the shortbread for 35 to 40 minutes, until the top and bottom are a light golden color.

Let the shortbread cool in the pan on a wire rack until the shortbread is warm. Do not allow it to cool completely. Sprinkle the shortbread with the remaining 2 tablespoons (26 g) of sugar and rose petals. Tilt the pan so that the sugar coats the entire surface of the shortbread evenly. Lift the shortbread from the pan and, with a sharp knife, cut the shortbread into 1-inch (2.5-cm)-thick bars. Allow the bars to cool completely before serving.

PLUM BLOSSOM "WINDOW" COOKIES

There will always be cookies that are "almost too pretty to eat," and there will always be those that are "*definitely* too pretty to eat." These plum blossom cookies are the latter. I make these cookies more often as decorative pieces (like ornaments for a Christmas tree!) than for eating. These cookies are a classic shortbread cookie with cutouts to create a "window." Isomalt, a sugar substitute derived from beets that is commonly used by sugar artists to create sugar sculptures and cake decorations, fills the cutouts to create a glass-like window set with winter plum blossoms. Alternatively, you can melt clear candies (like mints or Jolly Ranchers) to fill the cutouts if you cannot find isomalt crystals.

Yields 24 cookies

½ cup (113 g) unsalted butter, at room temperature

½ cup (60 g) powdered sugar

2 tsp (10 ml) pure vanilla extract

¾ tsp salt

1 cup (120 g) all-purpose flour

1 cup (240 g) isomalt crystals

2 tbsp (30 ml) water

Plum blossoms, for decorating (for a tutorial on how to press and dry blossoms, go to page 146)

In the bowl of a stand mixer fitted with a paddle attachment, beat the butter on low speed until it is smooth, about 1 minute. Add the powdered sugar, vanilla, and salt. Mix until the ingredients are combined, about 1 minute. While the mixer is running, add the flour and mix just until the dough is uniform in texture.

Gather the dough into a ball and flatten it into a disk. Wrap the disk in plastic wrap and chill the dough in the refrigerator for at least 1 hour to prevent the cookies from spreading in the oven.

Preheat the oven to 350°F (177°C). Line a large baking sheet with parchment paper.

Lightly flour a work surface. Roll out the dough into a rectangle that is about ¼ inch (6 mm) thick.

With a cookie cutter, cut the dough into the desired shapes and transfer the cookies to the prepared baking sheet. Using a smaller cookie cutter, create a cutout in the center of each cookie, leaving a ½-inch (13-mm) border of dough on each side of the "frame." Transfer the cookies to the prepared baking sheet, spacing them 2 inches (5 cm) apart.

Bake the cookies for 10 to 12 minutes, until they are golden around the edges. The exact baking time will vary depending on the size of the cookie and the thickness of the cutout, so keep a close eye on them. Allow the cookies to cool on the baking sheet for 10 minutes before transferring them to a wire rack to cool completely.

While the cookies are cooling, reduce the oven's temperature to 265°F (129°C). Place the isomalt in a small oven-safe pot over medium heat and allow the crystals to melt without stirring them.

Once the isomalt is boiling, remove the pot from the heat. The isomalt will be very bubbly. Keep the pot off of the heat until the bubbles settle down, about 15 seconds. Once the bubbles have settled down, return the pot to the heat and stir in the water, a little at a time. Steam will aggressively come off of the isomalt and it will still be very bubbly.

Place the pot in the oven for 10 minutes to reduce the number of air bubbles in the isomalt. (If you skip this step, the bubbles will stay in the isomalt and it will harden with air pockets in the cookies' windows.)

Meanwhile, line a baking sheet with a clean sheet of parchment paper. Transfer the cooled cookies to the prepared baking sheet. Place a plum blossom in the center cutout of each cookie.

Carefully remove the pot from the oven and use the isomalt while it is still hot. If the isomalt starts to thicken, place it back in the oven for 2 to 3 minutes, until it liquefies again.

With a small spoon, carefully pour a small amount of isomalt into the cutouts, using the spoon to spread out the isomalt as thinly as possible. Allow the isomalt to cool completely, about 15 minutes, before removing the cookies from the baking sheet.

*See photo on page 50.

 Note: To turn these into holiday ornaments, use a straw to punch out a hole in one corner of the cookies before baking. After baking, tie the cookies with a ribbon to hang them.

Choux

There are only so many things I am certain of, and among them are that you should always have at least two blocks of unsalted butter in the refrigerator, a dessert always needs salt, and choux is one of the most magical things that one can bake. Choux is a simple combination of milk, water, sugar, flour, and eggs—but the combination is a very precise one. Every time I see choux rise and hollow out in the oven, I am reminded of how magical baking really is. After the choux buns are baked, they can be filled with whatever your heart desires. Jasmine and Honey Éclairs (page 89), Chamomile-Mango Cream Puffs (page 79), and Chocolate-Lavender Religieuse (page 91) are just some of my favorite choux creations that are on rotation right now.

In order to make the perfect choux, the amount of each ingredient has to be quite precise, so I recommend using a kitchen scale to weigh the ingredients. Once the choux batter is made, it can be piped into mounds for cream puffs and religieuse, rows for éclairs, and rings for Paris-Brest.

Note: Cream puffs should be served the day they are filled or the choux bun will absorb the moisture from the filling and get very soft.

WHIPPED CHERRY BLOSSOM GANACHE *and* MATCHA CREAM PUFFS

I often dream of visiting Japan in the springtime when all the cherry blossoms are in full bloom and the streets are covered in a blanket of soft pink petals. These cream puffs pair cherry blossom powder with another Japanese ingredient I always find myself reaching for when I bake—matcha. Cherry blossom powder can be found in Japanese grocery stores and online. It adds a gentle floral flavor to desserts as well as an incredible deep pink color.

Yields 10 to 12 cream puffs

Whipped Cherry Blossom Ganache
2/3 cup (117 g) coarsely chopped white chocolate

1 cup (240 ml) heavy cream

3 tbsp (20 g) cherry blossom powder

Craquelin
4 tbsp (20 g) all-purpose flour

2 tbsp (26 g) brown sugar

2 tbsp (28 g) unsalted butter, softened

Pâte à Choux
1/4 cup (60 ml) water

1/4 cup (60 ml) whole milk

1/2 tsp granulated sugar

1/2 tsp salt

4 tbsp (56 g) unsalted butter

1/2 cup (60 g) plus 2 tbsp (10 g) all-purpose flour

4 oz (110 g) eggs, lightly beaten (see note on page 78)

Make the whipped cherry blossom ganache. Place the white chocolate into a medium heatproof bowl.

In a small saucepan over medium heat, bring the heavy cream to a boil. Pour the cream over the chocolate and let the mixture sit for 2 minutes. Whisk the chocolate until it is thoroughly melted and combined with the cream. Cover the ganache with plastic wrap and chill it in the refrigerator for at least 4 hours.

Transfer the chilled ganache to the bowl of a stand mixer fitted with a whisk attachment. Whisk the ganache on medium-high speed for 2 to 3 minutes, until it is light and fluffy. Add the cherry blossom powder and mix until the ingredients are combined. Cover the mixer bowl with plastic wrap and keep the whipped ganache in the refrigerator until you are ready to use it.

Make the craquelin. In a medium bowl, combine the flour, brown sugar, and butter and mix with a rubber spatula until the ingredients are smooth.

Lightly flour a work surface and line a large baking sheet with parchment paper. Roll out the craquelin dough until it is 1/8 inch (3 mm) thick. Use a 2-inch (5-cm) cookie cutter to cut out 12 dough circles. Transfer the dough circles to the prepared baking sheet and chill the cutouts in the refrigerator until they are ready to be used.

Make the pâte à choux. Preheat the oven to 350°F (177°C). Line a large baking sheet with parchment paper.

In a small saucepan over medium heat, combine the water, milk, granulated sugar, salt, and butter. Bring the mixture to a light boil, remove it from the heat, and immediately add all the flour at once. Quickly stir in the flour using a rubber spatula, then place the saucepan over medium-high heat.

(Continued)

WHIPPED CHERRY BLOSSOM GANACHE AND MATCHA CREAM PUFFS *(Continued)*

Matcha Whipped Cream
1 cup (240 ml) heavy cream
3 tbsp (24 g) powdered sugar
1 tbsp (6 g) matcha powder

Garnish
Powdered sugar, as needed

Note: While it may seem unusual to weigh eggs, a good rule of thumb is that 4 ounces (110 g) of eggs is equal to about 2½ large eggs.

Continue to stir the mixture for 1 to 2 minutes, without stopping, until the paste is smooth. It will pull away from the sides of the saucepan and leave a thin coating of cooked paste on the bottom when it is ready. The texture should resemble dry mashed potatoes.

Transfer the paste to the bowl of a stand mixer fitted with a paddle attachment. Mix on low speed for 3 to 5 minutes to allow the choux to cool down. Increase the mixer's speed to medium and gradually stream in the eggs. Mix for 1 to 2 minutes, until the ingredients are well combined.

Fit a piping bag with a large round piping tip. Transfer the pâte à choux to the prepared piping bag. Pipe out 12 choux mounds onto the prepared baking sheet, leaving roughly 2 inches (5 cm) between each puff. Add the craquelin to the tops of the choux mounds.

Bake the choux puffs for 35 minutes. Rotate the baking sheet and reduce the oven's temperature to 325°F (163°C), then bake the puffs for 10 minutes, or until they are a deep golden color. Remove the baking sheet from the oven and set it on a cooling rack.

Make the matcha whipped cream. In the bowl of a stand mixer fitted with a whisk attachment, whisk the heavy cream on high speed for 2 to 3 minutes, until medium-stiff peaks form. Add the powdered sugar and matcha powder and whip until they are combined. Transfer the matcha whipped cream to a piping bag fitted with a large star piping tip.

To assemble the cream puffs, cut off the top of the choux. Transfer the whipped cherry blossom ganache to a pastry bag fitted with a medium round pastry tip. Pipe the whipped cherry blossom ganache into the choux until it reaches the brim of the choux. Pipe 2 layers of the matcha whipped cream on top of the whipped cherry blossom ganache. Top the cream puff with the top of the choux, like a hat. Dust the choux with the powdered sugar.

CHAMOMILE-MANGO CREAM PUFFS

Because chamomile has such earthy floral notes, I often like to pair it with a bright and sweet fruit, like I do in my Chamomile Cake with Peach and Mascarpone Buttercream (page 17). These cream puffs are filled with a tangy mango and lemon curd before being topped with a lightly sweetened chamomile whipped cream.

Yields 10 to 12 cream puffs

Craquelin
4 tbsp (20 g) all-purpose flour

2 tbsp (26 g) brown sugar

2 tbsp (28 g) unsalted butter, softened

Pâte à Choux
¼ cup (60 ml) water

¼ cup (60 ml) whole milk

½ tsp granulated sugar

½ tsp salt

4 tbsp (56 g) unsalted butter

½ cup (60 g) plus 2 tbsp (10 g) all-purpose flour

4 oz (110 g) eggs, lightly beaten (see note)

Note: While it may seem unusual to weigh eggs, a good rule of thumb is that 4 ounces (110 g) of eggs is equal to about 2½ large eggs.

Make the craquelin. In a medium bowl, combine the flour, brown sugar, and butter and mix with a rubber spatula until the ingredients are smooth.

Lightly flour a work surface and line a large baking sheet with parchment paper. Roll out the craquelin dough until it is ⅛ inch (3 mm) thick. Use a 2-inch (5-cm) cookie cutter to cut out 12 dough circles. Transfer the dough circles to the prepared baking sheet and chill the cutouts in the refrigerator until they are ready to be used.

Make the pâte à choux. Preheat the oven to 350°F (177°C). Line a large baking sheet with parchment paper.

In a small saucepan over medium heat, combine the water, milk, granulated sugar, salt, and butter. Bring the mixture to a light boil, remove the saucepan from the heat, and immediately add all of the flour at once. Quickly stir in the flour using a rubber spatula, then place the saucepan over medium-high heat.

Continue to stir the mixture for 1 to 2 minutes, without stopping, until the paste is smooth. It will pull away from the sides of the saucepan and leave a thin coating of cooked paste on the bottom when it is ready. The texture should resemble dry mashed potatoes.

Transfer the paste to the bowl of a stand mixer fitted with a paddle attachment. Mix on low speed for 3 to 5 minutes to allow the choux to cool down. Increase the mixer's speed to medium and gradually stream in the eggs. Mix for 1 to 2 minutes, until the ingredients are well combined.

Fit a piping bag with a large round piping tip. Transfer the pâte à choux to the prepared piping bag. Pipe out 12 choux mounds onto the prepared baking sheet, leaving roughly 2 inches (5 cm) between each puff. Add the craquelin to the tops of the choux mounds.

Bake the choux puffs for 35 minutes. Rotate the baking sheet and reduce the oven's temperature to 325°F (163°C), then bake the puffs for 10 minutes, or until they are a deep golden color. Remove the baking sheet from the oven and set it on a cooling rack.

(Continued)

CHAMOMILE-MANGO CREAM PUFFS *(Continued)*

Mango Curd

1 large ripe mango, peeled and finely diced

½ cup (120 ml) fresh lemon juice

½ tsp salt

¾ cup (150 g) granulated sugar, divided

1 tsp pure vanilla extract

3 large egg yolks

1 large egg

½ cup (113 g) cold unsalted butter, cut into pieces

Chamomile Whipped Cream

1¼ cups (300 ml) heavy cream

4 to 5 bags chamomile tea

1 tsp pure vanilla extract

¼ cup (30 g) powdered sugar

Optional Garnishes

Royal Icing Glaze (page 86), as needed

Fresh chamomile flowers, gold leaf, or sprinkles, as needed

Powdered sugar, as needed

Make the mango curd. Place the mango in a medium saucepan. Whisk in the lemon juice, salt, ½ cup (100 g) of the granulated sugar, and vanilla. Bring the mixture to a simmer over medium heat, stirring to dissolve the sugar.

Meanwhile, in a medium bowl, whisk together the egg yolks, egg, and remaining ¼ cup (50 g) of the granulated sugar until the mixture is no longer grainy and is slightly lightened in color, about 2 minutes.

Whisking constantly, very gradually stream about half of the hot mango mixture into the egg mixture. Gradually whisk the mango-egg mixture back into the saucepan. Cook the mango curd over medium heat for 5 to 7 minutes, whisking constantly, until the curd thickens and the whisk leaves a visible trail (do not let it boil). Remove the saucepan from the heat and add the butter a couple of pieces at a time, whisking until it is incorporated before adding more. Strain the mango curd through a fine-mesh sieve and cover it with plastic wrap. Refrigerate the mango curd until it is cold.

Make the chamomile whipped cream. In a medium saucepan, combine the heavy cream and bags of chamomile tea. Heat the cream over medium heat until it reaches a simmer. Remove the saucepan from the heat. Allow the chamomile tea to steep for 15 to 20 minutes, until the cream is very fragrant. Remove the bags of chamomile tea and allow the cream to return to room temperature. Transfer the room-temperature cream to the refrigerator to chill for at least 2 hours.

Transfer the chamomile cream to the bowl of a stand mixer fitted with a whisk attachment. Add the vanilla. Whisk the mixture on high speed for 2 to 3 minutes, until medium-stiff peaks form. Add the powdered sugar and whisk on medium speed for 30 seconds to incorporate. Transfer the chamomile whipped cream to a piping bag fitted with a large star pastry tip.

To assemble the cream puffs, cut off the top of the choux with a serrated knife. Pipe the chilled mango curd into the choux until it almost reaches the brim. Pipe two layers of the chamomile whipped cream on top of the mango curd. Top the cream puff with the top of the choux, like a hat.

If you would like to garnish the cream puffs, dip the little choux hats in the Royal Icing Glaze and add any decorations (e.g., fresh chamomile flowers, gold leaf, or sprinkles) before topping the cream puffs, or dust the tops with the powdered sugar.

JASMINE-BLUEBERRY ICE CREAM CHOUX PUFFS

Choux will always be one of my favorite things to make, no matter what season it is. The season, though, might influence what goes inside the puff. In the summertime, I will often swap the whipped ganache filling for ice cream. These choux puffs are filled with a jasmine ice cream studded with blueberries. Both the ice cream custard base and most ice cream makers need to be chilled overnight before use, so keep that in mind when making ice cream!

Yields 10 to 12 choux puffs

Jasmine-Blueberry Ice Cream
1¾ cups (420 ml) heavy cream

1 cup (240 ml) whole milk

⅔ cup (133 g) granulated sugar, divided

¼ tsp salt

1 tsp pure vanilla extract

½ tsp jasmine extract

5 large egg yolks

¾ cup (75 g) fresh blueberries, divided

Craquelin
4 tbsp (20 g) all-purpose flour

2 tbsp (26 g) brown sugar

2 tbsp (28 g) unsalted butter, softened

Make the jasmine-blueberry ice cream. In a medium saucepan over medium heat, combine the heavy cream, milk, ⅓ cup (66 g) of granulated sugar, and salt. Add the vanilla and jasmine. Bring the mixture just to a simmer, stirring to dissolve the sugar. Remove the saucepan from the heat.

In a medium bowl, whisk together the egg yolks and the remaining ⅓ cup (66 g) of granulated sugar until the mixture is pale, about 2 minutes. Gradually whisk in ½ cup (120 ml) of the warm cream mixture. Whisk the yolk mixture into the remaining cream mixture. Cook the mixture over medium heat for 2 to 3 minutes, stirring constantly, until it is thick enough to coat a wooden spoon.

Strain the custard through a fine-mesh sieve into a medium bowl set over a bowl of ice water. Tightly cover the bowl with plastic wrap and transfer it to the refrigerator to cool completely. Process the chilled custard in an ice cream maker according to the manufacturer's instructions. While the ice cream is churning, add half of the blueberries to the ice cream churner (they will add some color to the ice cream base). Once churning is complete, fold the remaining blueberries into the ice cream. Transfer the ice cream to an airtight container and cover it. Freeze the ice cream until it is firm, at least 4 hours.

Make the craquelin. In a medium bowl, combine the flour, brown sugar, and butter and mix with a rubber spatula until they are smooth.

Lightly flour a work surface and line a large baking sheet with parchment paper. Roll out the craquelin dough until it is ⅛ inch (3 mm) thick. Use a 2-inch (5-cm) cookie cutter to cut out 12 dough circles. Transfer the dough circles to the prepared baking sheet and chill the cutouts in the refrigerator until they are ready to be used.

(Continued)

JASMINE-BLUEBERRY ICE CREAM CHOUX PUFFS
(Continued)

Pâte à Choux
¼ cup (60 ml) water

¼ cup (60 ml) whole milk

½ tsp granulated sugar

½ tsp salt

4 tbsp (56 g) unsalted butter

½ cup (60 g) plus 2 tbsp (10 g) all-purpose flour

4 oz (110 g) eggs, lightly beaten (see note)

Garnish
Powdered sugar, as needed

Make the pâte à choux. Preheat the oven to 350°F (177°C). Line a large baking sheet with parchment paper.

In a small saucepan over medium heat, combine the water, milk, granulated sugar, salt, and butter. Bring the mixture to a light boil, remove the saucepan from the heat, and immediately add all of the flour at once. Quickly stir in the flour using a rubber spatula, then place the saucepan over medium-high heat.

Continue to stir the mixture for 1 to 2 minutes, without stopping, until the paste is smooth and shiny. It will pull away from the sides of the saucepan and leave a thin coating of cooked paste on the bottom when it is ready. The texture should resemble dry mashed potatoes.

Transfer the paste to the bowl of a stand mixer fitted with a paddle attachment. Mix on low speed for 3 to 5 minutes to allow the choux to cool down. Increase the mixer's speed to medium and gradually stream in the eggs. Mix for 1 to 2 minutes, until the ingredients are well combined.

Fit a piping bag with a large round piping tip. Transfer the pâte à choux to the prepared piping bag. Pipe out 12 choux mounds onto the prepared baking sheet, leaving roughly 2 inches (5 cm) between each puff. Add the craquelin to the tops of the choux mounds.

Bake the choux puffs for 35 minutes. Rotate the baking sheet and reduce the oven's temperature to 325°F (163°C), then bake the puffs for 10 minutes, or until they are a deep golden color. Remove the baking sheet from the oven and set it on a cooling rack.

To assemble the puffs, cut off the top of the choux with a serrated knife. Place a generous scoop of ice cream inside the puff. Top the ice cream with the top of choux, like a hat. Dust the choux puffs with the powdered sugar.

Note: While it may seem unusual to weigh eggs, a good rule of thumb is that 4 ounces (110 g) of eggs is equal to about 2½ large eggs.

COFFEE *and* MILK CHOCOLATE CREAM PUFFS *with* CANDIED ROSE PETALS

I always take my coffee black, but once a year during the holidays, I like to treat myself to a floral-flavored mocha. These cream puffs are an ode to my favorite festive holiday drink. Each cream puff is filled with whipped milk chocolate, topped with coffee whipped cream, and garnished with a sparkling sugared rose petal.

Yields 10 to 12 cream puffs

Whipped Milk Chocolate Ganache
2/3 cup (117 g) coarsely chopped milk chocolate

1 cup (240 ml) heavy cream

1/4 tsp salt

Craquelin
4 tbsp (20 g) all-purpose flour

2 tbsp (26 g) brown sugar

2 tbsp (28 g) unsalted butter, softened

Pâte à Choux
1/4 cup (60 ml) water

1/4 cup (60 ml) whole milk

1/2 tsp granulated sugar

1/2 tsp salt

4 tbsp (56 g) unsalted butter

1/2 cup (60 g) plus 2 tbsp (10 g) all-purpose flour

4 oz (110 g) eggs, lightly beaten (see note on page 86)

Make the whipped milk chocolate ganache. Place the chocolate in a medium heatproof bowl. In a small saucepan over medium heat, bring the heavy cream to a boil. Pour the cream over the chocolate and let the mixture sit for 1 minute. Add the salt. Whisk the chocolate until it is thoroughly melted and combined with the cream. Cover the bowl with plastic wrap and transfer the bowl to the refrigerator to chill the ganache for at least 4 hours.

Once the ganache is chilled and ready to use, transfer it to the bowl of a stand mixer fitted with a whisk attachment. Whisk the ganache on medium-high speed for 2 to 3 minutes, until it is light and fluffy. Transfer the ganache to a piping bag fitted with a round pastry tip.

Make the craquelin. In a medium bowl, combine the flour, brown sugar, and butter and mix with a rubber spatula until the ingredients are smooth.

Lightly flour a work surface and line a large baking sheet with parchment paper. Roll out the craquelin dough until it is 1/8 inch (3 mm) thick. Use a 2-inch (5-cm) cookie cutter to cut out 12 dough circles. Transfer the dough circles to the prepared baking sheet and chill the cutouts in the refrigerator until they are ready to be used.

Make the pâte à choux. Preheat the oven to 350°F (177°C). Line a large baking sheet with parchment paper.

In a small saucepan over medium heat, combine the water, milk, granulated sugar, salt, and butter. Bring the mixture to a light boil, remove the saucepan from the heat, and immediately add all the flour at once. Quickly stir in the flour using a rubber spatula, then place the saucepan over medium-high heat.

Continue to stir the mixture for 1 to 2 minutes, without stopping, until the paste is smooth and shiny. It will pull away from the sides of the saucepan and leave a thin coating of cooked paste on the bottom when it is ready. The texture should resemble dry mashed potatoes.

(Continued)

COFFEE AND MILK CHOCOLATE CREAM PUFFS
WITH CANDIED ROSE PETALS *(Continued)*

Coffee Whipped Cream
1¼ cups (300 ml) heavy cream

1 oz (30 ml) prepared espresso or
1 tsp espresso powder

2 tsp (10 ml) pure vanilla extract

Royal Icing Glaze
¾ cup (90 g) powdered sugar

1 tbsp (15 ml) whole milk or water

¼ tsp pure vanilla extract

¼ tsp culinary-grade rose water

Garnish
Candied rose petals, as needed
(page 145)

Transfer the paste to the bowl of a stand mixer fitted with a paddle attachment. Mix on low speed for 3 to 5 minutes to allow the choux to cool down. Increase the mixer's speed to medium and gradually stream in the eggs. Mix for 1 to 2 minutes, until the ingredients are well combined.

Fit a piping bag with a large round piping tip. Transfer the pâte à choux to the prepared piping bag. Pipe out 12 choux mounds onto the prepared baking sheet, leaving roughly 2 inches (5 cm) between each puff. Add the craquelin to the tops of the choux mounds.

Bake the choux puffs for 35 minutes. Rotate the baking sheet and reduce the oven's temperature to 325°F (163°C), then bake the puffs for 10 minutes, or until the choux are a deep golden color. Remove the baking sheet from the oven and set it on a cooling rack.

Make the coffee whipped cream. In a stand mixer fitted with a whisk attachment, whisk the heavy cream on high speed for 2 to 3 minutes, until medium-stiff peaks form. Add the espresso and vanilla. Whip until they are incorporated.

To assemble the cream puffs, cut off the top of the choux with a serrated knife. Pipe the whipped milk chocolate ganache into the choux until it reaches the brim. Pipe two layers of coffee whipped cream on top of the ganache.

Make the royal icing glaze. In a small bowl, whisk together the powdered sugar, milk, vanilla, and rose water. To garnish the cream puffs, dip the craquelin "hats" in the royal icing glaze and adhere a candied rose petal to them. Place the hats on top of the cream puffs.

Note: While it may seem unusual to weigh eggs, a good rule of thumb is that 4 ounces (110 g) of eggs is equal to about 2½ large eggs.

JASMINE *and* HONEY ÉCLAIRS

Éclairs start the same way cream puffs do, by making a choux pastry and topping each portion of dough with a cookie-like crust. The craquelin crust is optional but adds so much more flavor and texture to each choux pastry. What differentiates an éclair from a cream puff is the shape in which it's piped. For éclairs, choux dough is piped into a log instead of a mound. Éclairs are baked in a similar fashion, starting at a higher temperature and then changing to a lower temperature to ensure the center of each pastry is cooked through. Once cooled, these éclairs are filled with the most luscious whipped jasmine-honey ganache and topped with a simple glaze and edible flower.

Yields 6 to 8 éclairs

Whipped Jasmine-Honey Ganache
1⅓ cups (320 ml) heavy cream

½ cup (12 g) dried culinary-grade jasmine flowers

⅔ cup (117 g) coarsely chopped white chocolate

2 tbsp (30 ml) honey

Craquelin
4 tbsp (20 g) all-purpose flour

2 tbsp (26 g) brown sugar

2 tbsp (28 g) unsalted butter, softened

Pâte à Choux
¼ cup (60 ml) water

¼ cup (60 ml) whole milk

½ tsp granulated sugar

½ tsp salt

4 tbsp (56 g) unsalted butter

½ cup (60 g) plus 2 tbsp (10 g) all-purpose flour

4 oz (110 g) eggs, lightly beaten (see note on page 90)

Optional Garnishes
Royal icing glaze, as needed (page 86)

Fresh culinary-grade edible flowers, as needed

Make the whipped jasmine-honey ganache. In a medium saucepan over medium heat, combine the heavy cream and jasmine flowers. Heat the mixture for about 2 minutes, until it reaches a light simmer. Allow the jasmine to steep in the heavy cream for 15 to 20 minutes, until it is very fragrant. Strain the cream through a fine-mesh sieve to remove the flowers.

Place the white chocolate in a medium heatproof bowl. Pour the cream over the white chocolate. Allow the mixture to sit for 1 minute so the white chocolate melts. Whisk the mixture until the white chocolate has fully melted and is combined with the cream. Cover the mixture with plastic wrap and chill it in the refrigerator for at least 4 hours.

Transfer the chilled ganache to the bowl of a stand mixer fitted with a whisk attachment. Whisk the ganache on medium-high speed for 2 to 3 minutes, until it is light and fluffy. Reduce the mixer's speed to low, then gradually add the honey and whisk until the ingredients are combined. Cover the stand mixer bowl with plastic wrap and place the whipped ganache in the refrigerator until you are ready to use it.

Make the craquelin. In a medium bowl, combine the flour, brown sugar, and butter and mix with a rubber spatula until the ingredients are smooth.

Lightly flour a work surface and line a large baking sheet with parchment paper. Roll out the craquelin dough until it is ⅛ inch (3 mm) thick. Using a knife, cut the craquelin into strips that are about 1 inch (2.5 cm) wide and 4 to 5 inches (10 to 13 cm) long. Transfer the strips to the prepared baking sheet and chill them in the refrigerator until they are ready to be used.

Make the pâte à choux. Preheat the oven to 350°F (177°C). Line a large baking sheet with parchment paper.

(Continued)

JASMINE AND HONEY ÉCLAIRS *(Continued)*

In a small saucepan over medium heat, combine the water, milk, granulated sugar, salt, and butter. Bring the mixture to a light boil, remove the saucepan from the heat, and immediately add all of the flour at once. Quickly stir in the flour using a rubber spatula, then place the saucepan over medium-high heat.

Continue to stir the mixture for 1 to 2 minutes, without stopping, until the paste is smooth. It will pull away from the sides of the saucepan and leave a thin coating of cooked paste on the bottom when it is ready. The texture should resemble dry mashed potatoes.

Transfer the paste to the bowl of a stand mixer fitted with a paddle attachment. Mix on low speed for 3 to 5 minutes to allow the choux to cool down. Increase the mixer's speed to medium and gradually stream in the eggs. Mix for 1 to 2 minutes, until the ingredients are well combined.

Fit a piping bag with a large round piping tip. Transfer the pâte à choux to the prepared piping bag. Pipe out rows of choux mounds that are 4 to 5 inches (10 to 13 cm) in length onto the prepared baking sheet, leaving roughly 2 inches (5 cm) between each row. Add the craquelin to the top of each piped choux.

Bake the choux for 25 minutes. Rotate the baking sheet and reduce the oven's temperature to 325°F (163°C), then bake the choux for 10 minutes, or until they are a deep golden color. Remove the baking sheet from the oven and set it on a cooling rack.

Transfer the whipped ganache to a pastry bag fitted with an open star piping tip. Using a sharp serrated knife, cut the éclairs lengthwise on a horizontal plane. Pipe the ganache in a zigzag pattern until the éclair is filled. Top the ganache with the other half of the éclair.

If desired, garnish the éclairs. Dip the top of each éclair into the royal icing glaze before placing the top on the piped ganache, and place an edible flower on the glaze.

 Note: While it may seem unusual to weigh eggs, a good rule of thumb is that 4 ounces (110 g) of eggs is equal to about 2½ large eggs.

CHOCOLATE-LAVENDER RELIGIEUSE

Religieuse are usually filled with a *crème pâtissière* (pastry cream) and have a piped whipped cream collar where the two puffs meet. These religieuse pastries are filled with a dark chocolate-lavender pastry cream, glazed with chocolate ganache, and topped with edible gold leaf for extra sparkle. This recipe has many different components, but thankfully the tasks can be divided between two days. I like to make the pastry cream the night before, so it has sufficient time to chill in the refrigerator, and to make the choux and assemble the pastries the day I am serving them.

Yields 5 to 7 religieuse

Dark Chocolate-Lavender Pastry Cream

6 large egg yolks

7 tbsp (91 g) granulated sugar

1½ tbsp (8 g) all-purpose flour

1½ tbsp (12 g) cornstarch

2 ⅔ cups (640 ml) whole milk

1 ⅓ cups (320 ml) heavy cream

1 ¼ cups (220 g) coarsely chopped dark chocolate

¾ tsp dried culinary-grade lavender, finely ground

Craquelin

4 tbsp (20 g) all-purpose flour

2 tbsp (26 g) brown sugar

2 tbsp (28 g) unsalted butter, softened

Pâte à Choux

¼ cup (60 ml) water

¼ cup (60 ml) whole milk

½ tsp granulated sugar

½ tsp salt

4 tbsp (56 g) unsalted butter

½ cup (60 g) plus 2 tbsp (10 g) all-purpose flour

4 oz (110 g) eggs, lightly beaten (see note)

Make the dark chocolate-lavender pastry cream. In a large bowl, whisk together the egg yolks, granulated sugar, flour, and cornstarch. Set the mixture aside.

In a large saucepan over medium heat, bring the milk and heavy cream to a simmer. While whisking vigorously, slowly pour ½ cup (120 ml) of the hot milk mixture into the egg mixture. Whisk the egg-milk mixture back into the saucepan. Cook the pastry cream over low heat for 3 to 5 minutes, whisking constantly, until it is thick. Turn off the heat and add the dark chocolate, whisking until it has melted. Whisk in the lavender. Transfer the pastry cream to a large bowl, cover the bowl with plastic wrap, and refrigerate the pastry cream until it is cool, about 2 hours.

Make the craquelin. In a medium bowl, combine the flour, brown sugar, and butter and mix with a rubber spatula until the ingredients are smooth.

Lightly flour a work surface and line a large baking sheet with parchment paper. Roll out the craquelin dough until it is ⅛ inch (3 mm) thick. Use a 2-inch (5-cm) cookie cutter to cut out 6 dough circles and a 1-inch (2.5-cm) cookie cutter to cut out another 6 dough circles. Transfer the dough circles to the prepared baking sheet and chill the cutouts until they are ready to be used.

Make the pâte à choux. Preheat the oven to 350°F (177°C). Line a large baking sheet with parchment paper.

In a small saucepan over medium heat, combine the water, milk, granulated sugar, salt, and butter. Bring the mixture to a light boil, remove the saucepan from the heat, and immediately add all of the flour at once. Quickly stir in the flour using a rubber spatula, then place the saucepan over medium-high heat.

(Continued)

CHOCOLATE-LAVENDER RELIGIEUSE *(Continued)*

Chocolate Ganache
2/3 cup (117 g) coarsely chopped dark chocolate

1/2 cup (120 ml) heavy cream

Whipped Cream
3/4 cup (180 ml) heavy cream

1 tsp pure vanilla extract

Garnish
Edible gold leaf, as needed

Note: While it may seem unusual to weigh eggs, a good rule of thumb is that 4 ounces (110 g) of eggs is equal to about 2½ large eggs.

Continue to stir the mixture for 1 to 2 minutes, without stopping, until the paste is smooth. It will pull away from the sides of the saucepan and leave a thin coating of cooked paste on the bottom when it is ready. The texture should resemble dry mashed potatoes.

Transfer the paste to the bowl of a stand mixer fitted with a paddle attachment. Mix on low speed for 3 to 5 minutes to allow the choux to cool down. Increase the mixer's speed to medium and gradually stream in the eggs. Mix for 1 to 2 minutes, until the ingredients are well combined.

Fit a piping bag with a large round piping tip. Transfer the pâte à choux to the prepared piping bag. Pipe six 1½-inch (4-cm) and six 1-inch (2.5-cm) choux mounds onto the prepared baking sheet, leaving roughly 2 inches (5 cm) between each puff. Add the craquelin to the top of the choux mounds, placing the larger craquelin cutouts on the larger choux mounds.

Bake the choux puffs for 25 minutes. Rotate the baking sheet and reduce the oven's temperature to 325°F (163°C), then bake the choux for 10 to 15 minutes, or until they are a deep golden color. Remove the baking sheet from the oven and set it on a cooling rack.

Make the chocolate ganache. Place the dark chocolate in a medium heatproof bowl. Heat the heavy cream in a small saucepan over medium heat until it begins to simmer gently. Pour the cream over the chocolate, then let the mixture sit for 2 minutes, until the chocolate has softened. With a whisk, slowly stir until the chocolate and cream are completely combined and the chocolate has melted. Let the ganache cool and thicken for 15 to 20 minutes.

Make the whipped cream. In the bowl of a stand mixer fitted with a whisk attachment, combine the heavy cream and vanilla. Whisk on high speed for 2 to 3 minutes, until medium-stiff peaks form. At this point, the cream will have doubled in volume and will hold its shape on the end of the whisk. Transfer the whipped cream to a piping bag fitted with a small open star piping tip.

To assemble the religieuse, transfer the chilled pastry cream to a piping bag fitted with a medium round piping tip. With a chopstick or a straw, poke a hole at the bottom of each puff and fill it with pastry cream. Dip the top of each puff in the ganache. Place the smaller filled puff on top of the larger filled puff. Pipe a ring of whipped cream to create a "collar" where the two puffs meet.

To garnish the religieuse, sprinkle the top with the edible gold leaf.

*See photo on page 74.

Pies and Tarts

Pie crust was the one pastry I was most afraid of tackling when I first started baking, but it's so worth it. I now make traditional pie crust as often as I make a pâte sablée or graham cracker crust. The Strawberry, Rhubarb, and Rose Frangipane Tart (page 112) is one of my favorite recipes to make in the summertime, and I set aside a few hours in the afternoon to make my annual Apple-Rose Custard Tart (page 121) during apple season. The No-Bake Honey Blossom Cheesecake Tart with Plums (page 118) comes out to play during plum season, and there is no way I will miss the opportunity to make my Pear Pie with Pressed-Flower Crust (page 107) in early fall. Fruity pies and tarts are my love letters to their respective seasons, and adding a floral touch renders them even more romantic.

STRAWBERRY-ROSE PIE

Fruit pies are about abundance. There is an abundance of layers in a flaky pie crust, an abundance of fresh fruit in the filling, and an abundance of joy in making a pie lattice. There are few fruits that I enjoy working with more than strawberries, and this is especially true in the summertime. The strawberry filling in this pie is simple, but its flavors are nuanced. The fragrant sweetness of strawberries is layered with rose water and rounded out with the brightness of lemon.

Yields 1 (10-inch [25-cm]) double-crust pie

All-Butter Pie Crust

2½ cups (300 g) all-purpose flour

1 tbsp (13 g) granulated sugar

1 tsp salt

1 cup (227 g) very cold unsalted butter, cut into ½-inch (13-mm) pieces

½ cup (120 ml) cold water

½ cup (110 g) ice cubes

1 tbsp (15 ml) apple cider vinegar

1 large egg

1 tbsp (15 ml) whole milk

Strawberry-Rose Filling

6 cups (864 g) fresh strawberries, hulled and sliced in half

½ cup (100 g) granulated sugar (see note)

⅓ cup (67 g) packed brown sugar

⅓ cup (40 g) plus 2 tbsp (16 g) cornstarch

2 tbsp (30 ml) fresh lemon juice

1 tbsp (15 ml) culinary-grade rose water

¼ tsp salt

Make the all-butter pie crust. In a large bowl, stir together the flour, granulated sugar, and salt. Add the butter. With a pastry cutter or a fork, quickly cut the butter into the flour mixture until mostly pea-size pieces of butter remain (a few larger pieces are okay).

In a large measuring cup or a small bowl, combine the water, ice, and vinegar. Sprinkle 2 tablespoons (15 ml) of the ice-water mixture over the flour mixture and mix with a spatula until the water is fully incorporated. Add more of the ice-water mixture, 1 to 2 tablespoons (15 to 30 ml) at a time. Using the spatula or your hands, mix until the dough comes together in a ball with some dry, shaggy bits remaining. Squeeze and pinch the dough with your fingertips to bring all the dough together, sprinkling dry bits with 1 to 2 tablespoons (15 to 30 ml) of the ice-water mixture, if necessary, to combine.

Divide the dough into 2 portions. Shape each portion of dough into a flat disk, wrap each disk in plastic, and refrigerate the dough for at least 1 hour (or overnight), to give the dough time to rest.

Preheat the oven to 400°F (204°C).

Make the strawberry-rose filling. In a large bowl, stir together the strawberries, granulated sugar, brown sugar, cornstarch, lemon juice, rose water, and salt. Allow the mixture to rest for at least 15 minutes while you roll out the dough.

On a lightly floured work surface, roll out one disk of the dough to create an 11½-inch (29-cm) circle. Fit the dough into a 10-inch (25-cm) pie dish. Roll out the second disk of dough to create an 11-inch (28-cm) circle.

To prepare the lattice, cut the second rolled-out disk of pie dough into ½- to 1-inch (13-mm to 2.5-cm)-wide strips, depending on how wide you want the lattice pieces to be. Set these strips aside. To create a braided strip, cut three ¼-inch (6-mm) strips of dough and braid as you would braid hair, pinching all three strips at the top and continuing to overlap the middle strip with the exterior strips.

(Continued)

STRAWBERRY-ROSE PIE *(Continued)*

Transfer the strawberry-rose filling to the pie dish (straining out the juices that have released). In a small bowl, whisk together the egg and milk to create an egg wash. Set the egg wash aside.

To assemble the lattice, place the longest strip of pie dough down the middle of the filled pie. Place the other strips of pie dough on both sides of the center strip, leaving a 1-inch (2.5-cm) gap between each strip, until you reach the edge of the pie. To create the woven lattice, lift up every other strip on the pie to the halfway mark. Place a new strip of pie dough perpendicular to the pieces already there. Take the pieces that were lifted up and place them over the new perpendicular piece. Repeat these steps with the pieces of dough that are now under the perpendicular piece. Repeat until you reach the edge of the pie and each piece of dough is in an over-under-over pattern. See photos on page 99.

Trim any pie dough hanging over the edges of the pie dish. Using the tines of a fork, press down on the perimeter of the pie, combining the top and bottom crusts at the edges.

Gather any leftover dough and roll it into a circle that is ¼ inch (6 mm) thick. Using a cookie cutter or stamp of your choice, cut out shapes from the pie dough. With a pastry brush or your fingers, brush a thin layer of the egg wash onto the backside of each cutout before arranging it on the lattice pie top. Egg wash the top of the pie.

Place the pie on a large rimmed baking sheet to catch any juices that might bubble over. Bake the pie on the baking sheet for 20 minutes. Reduce the oven's temperature to 350°F (177°C) and bake the pie for 35 to 45 minutes, or until the crust is golden brown and the filling begins to bubble through the lattice or vents. Let the pie cool on a wire rack for about 3 hours.

 Notes: If your strawberries are not completely ripe, you can add 2 tablespoons (26 g) more of granulated sugar to compensate.

The more intricate the lattice weave, the more pie dough you will need. If you know you will be making a very decorative lattice, make 1½ portions of pie dough.

PEACH GALETTE *with* LAVENDER WHIPPED CREAM

Galettes are the less-fussy version of pie with all the great components of a pie—a tender fruit filling, a flaky and buttery crust, and a crackly sugar layer on top of the pastry. I love making galettes on warmer days when I do not want to be handling pie crust for a lattice top and on days I need a fruit dessert in a pinch. My favorite thing about a galette? Seeing the fruit on display in all its glory. My favorite fruit to use during late summer and early fall is peaches. Use whatever fruit is in season, and I promise that you will not even miss pie.

Yields 1 (8-inch [20-cm]) galette

All-Butter Pie Crust

1¼ cups (150 g) all-purpose flour

1½ tsp (7 g) granulated sugar, plus more as needed

½ tsp salt

½ cup (113 g) very cold unsalted butter, cut into ½-inch (13-mm) pieces

½ cup (120 ml) cold water

½ cup (110 g) ice cubes

1 tbsp (15 ml) apple cider vinegar

1 large egg

1 tbsp (15 ml) water

Peach Filling

⅓ cup (67 g) granulated sugar

2 tsp (6 g) cornstarch

1 tsp finely grated lemon zest

½ tsp salt

1½ to 2 lbs (675 to 900 g) fresh peaches, cut into ¾-inch (19-mm)-thick wedges

1 tbsp (15 ml) fresh lemon juice

1 tsp pure vanilla extract

Make the all-butter pie crust. In a large bowl, stir together the flour, granulated sugar, and salt. Add the butter. With a pastry cutter or a fork, quickly cut the butter into the flour mixture until mostly pea-size pieces of butter remain (a few larger pieces are okay).

In a large measuring cup or a small bowl, combine the water, ice, and vinegar. Sprinkle 2 tablespoons (30 ml) of the ice-water mixture over the flour mixture and mix with a spatula until the water is fully incorporated. Add more of the ice-water mixture, 1 to 2 tablespoons (15 to 30 ml) at a time. Using the spatula or your hands, mix until the dough comes together in a ball with some dry, shaggy bits remaining. Squeeze and pinch the dough with your fingertips to bring all the dough together, sprinkling dry bits with more small splashes of the ice-water mixture, if necessary, to combine. Shape the dough into a flat disk, wrap it in plastic and refrigerate it for at least 1 hour (or overnight), to give the dough time to rest.

With a floured rolling pin, roll out the dough on a lightly floured surface to create a 12- to 14-inch (30- to 35-cm) circle that is about ⅛ inch (3 mm) thick (don't worry about cracks around the edges). If the dough sticks to the work surface, lift it on one side and scatter flour underneath before continuing. Transfer the rolled-out dough to a sheet of parchment paper. Slide the parchment paper onto a large rimmed baking sheet and chill the dough while you prepare the peach filling.

Preheat the oven to 375°F (191°C).

Make the peach filling. In a medium bowl, combine the granulated sugar, cornstarch, lemon zest, and salt. Toss to combine the ingredients, then add the peaches and toss to coat them in the mixture. Add the lemon juice and vanilla and toss gently to combine.

(Continued)

PEACH GALETTE WITH LAVENDER WHIPPED CREAM
(Continued)

Lavender Whipped Cream
1 cup (240 ml) heavy cream

¼ cup (30 g) powdered sugar

½ tsp dried culinary-grade lavender, finely ground

While the dough is still on the parchment paper on the rimmed baking sheet, arrange the peaches in the center of the dough and spread them out evenly, leaving a 3-inch (7.5-cm) border. Fold the edges of the dough up and over the fruit, pleating the edges as needed. If the edge of the dough tears, patch it with dough scraps and pinch to seal the galette.

In a small bowl, whisk together the egg and water to form an egg wash. Brush the egg wash all over the dough. Sprinkle additional granulated sugar or coarse sanding sugar evenly over the dough.

Bake the galette for 45 to 50 minutes, rotating it halfway through the baking time, until the crust is deep golden brown everywhere, the fruit is softened, and the juices are bubbling. Allow the galette to cool at least 1 hour before serving.

Make the lavender whipped cream. In the bowl of a stand mixer fitted with a whisk attachment, combine the heavy cream, powdered sugar, and lavender. Whisk the mixture on high speed for 2 to 3 minutes, until medium-stiff peaks form. Serve the lavender whipped cream with the cooled galette.

FLORAL HAND PIES

Hand pies are the perfect portable pastry. I would even say that they are one of the most perfect pastries, portability aside. They are my favorite treat to bring to picnics and potlucks because they do not require me to bring a knife or dessert plates to serve them, unlike a traditional pie or galette. These hand pies are made with a super flaky all-butter pie crust and a simple strawberry compote that comes together in ten minutes. Serve them plain or top them with a glaze and edible flowers.

Yields 8 to 10 (3-inch [8-cm]) hand pies

All-Butter Pie Crust

1¼ cups (150 g) all-purpose flour

1½ tsp (6 g) granulated sugar

½ tsp salt

½ cup (113 g) very cold unsalted butter, cut into ½-inch (13-mm) pieces

½ cup (120 ml) cold water

½ cup (110 g) ice cubes

1 tbsp (15 ml) apple cider vinegar

1 large egg

1 tablespoon (15 ml) water

Strawberry Filling

2½ cups (360 g) fresh strawberries, hulled and diced

3 tbsp (45 ml) fresh orange juice

2 tbsp (26 g) granulated sugar

¼ tsp salt

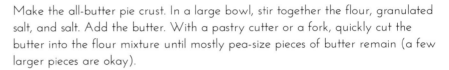

Make the all-butter pie crust. In a large bowl, stir together the flour, granulated salt, and salt. Add the butter. With a pastry cutter or a fork, quickly cut the butter into the flour mixture until mostly pea-size pieces of butter remain (a few larger pieces are okay).

In a large measuring cup or a small bowl, combine the water, ice, and vinegar. Sprinkle 2 tablespoons (30 ml) of the ice-water mixture over the flour mixture and mix with a spatula until the water is fully incorporated. Add more of the ice-water mixture, 1 to 2 tablespoons (15 to 30 ml) at a time. Using the spatula or your hands, mix until the dough comes together in a ball with some dry, shaggy bits remaining. Squeeze and pinch the dough with your fingertips to bring all the dough together, sprinkling dry bits with more small splashes of the ice-water mixture, if necessary, to combine.

Shape the dough into a flat disk, wrap it in plastic, and refrigerate the dough for at least 1 hour (or overnight), to give the dough time to rest.

Make the strawberry filling. In a medium saucepan over medium heat, combine the strawberries, orange juice, granulated sugar, and salt. Cook the mixture for about 10 minutes, stirring frequently, until some of the strawberries break down and some remain whole but soft. Remove the filling from the heat and allow it to cool.

Preheat the oven to 350°F (177°C). Line a large baking sheet with parchment paper.

On a floured work surface, roll out the disk of dough until it reaches ¼ inch (6 mm) in thickness. Using a 2- or 3-inch (5- or 7.5-cm) cookie cutter, stamp out an even number of circles. Place a large spoonful of the strawberry filling in the centers of half of the dough circles. Take a second dough circle and gently lay it on top of a filled circle. Using the tines of a fork, press down on the edges to seal the hand pie. Once all the hand pies have been sealed, use the fork to prick holes in the tops to allow steam to escape during baking. Transfer the hand pies to the prepared baking sheet.

(Continued)

FLORAL HAND PIES *(Continued)*

Royal Icing Glaze

3/4 cup (90 g) powdered sugar

1 tbsp (15 ml) whole milk or water

1/4 tsp pure vanilla extract

Gel food coloring, as needed
(optional)

Garnish

Fresh or dried culinary-grade edible
flowers, as needed (for a tutorial on
how to press and dry flowers, go to
page 146)

In a small bowl, whisk together the egg and water. Brush the egg wash on the hand pies.

Bake the hand pies for 24 to 28 minutes, until they are golden brown. Remove the hand pies from the oven and allow them to cool on the baking sheet for 10 minutes. Transfer the hand pies to a wire rack to cool completely.

Make the royal icing glaze. In a medium bowl, whisk together the powdered sugar, milk, vanilla, and food coloring (if using) until the glaze reaches a spreadable consistency. Add more milk if needed.

Using the back of a small spoon, spread a thin layer of the royal icing glaze on each cooled hand pie. To garnish the hand pies, arrange the edible flowers on top of the glaze before it sets.

PEAR PIE *with* PRESSED-FLOWER CRUST

This pie exists because I love making a beautiful lattice pie top more than anything else—maybe even more than eating the pie itself. The process of braiding and weaving a lattice top is so therapeutic. There is nothing else I would rather do, especially on a rainy fall day. Edible flowers are gently pressed onto the pie dough to take my love of lattice tops to the next level, while tender vanilla-scented pears fill the pie. This is a pie I will always keep in rotation during the crisp autumn months.

Yields 1 (10-inch [25-cm]) double-crust pie

All-Butter Pie Crust

2½ cups (300 g) all-purpose flour

1 tbsp (13 g) granulated sugar

1 tsp salt

1 cup (227 g) very cold unsalted butter, cut into ½-inch (13-mm) pieces

½ cup (120 ml) cold water

½ cup (110 g) ice cubes

1 tbsp (15 ml) apple cider vinegar

Fresh culinary-grade edible flowers, as needed

1 large egg

1 tbsp (15 ml) water

Coarse sanding sugar, as needed

Pear Filling

7 to 8 medium Bartlett or Anjou pears, peeled, cored, and cut into ½-inch (13-mm)-thick slices

½ cup (100 g) plus 2 tbsp (26 g) granulated sugar

2 tbsp (30 ml) fresh lemon juice

1 tbsp (15 ml) pure vanilla extract

½ cup (60 g) all-purpose flour

½ tsp ground cinnamon

¼ tsp salt

1 tbsp (14 g) unsalted butter, cut into small pieces

Make the all-butter pie crust. In a large bowl, stir together the flour, granulated sugar, and salt. Add the butter. With a pastry cutter or a fork, quickly cut the butter into the flour mixture until mostly pea-size pieces of butter remain (a few larger pieces are okay).

In a large measuring cup or a small bowl, combine the water, ice, and vinegar. Sprinkle 2 tablespoons (30 ml) of the ice-water mixture over the flour mixture and mix with a spatula until the water is fully incorporated. Add more of the ice-water mixture, 1 to 2 tablespoons (15 to 30 ml) at a time. Using the spatula or your hands, mix until the dough comes together in a ball with some dry, shaggy bits remaining. Squeeze and pinch the dough with your fingertips to bring all the dough together, sprinkling dry bits with more small splashes of the ice-water mixture, if necessary, to combine.

Divide the dough into two portions. Shape each portion of dough into a flat disk, wrap each disk in plastic, and refrigerate the dough for at least 1 hour (or overnight), to give the dough time to rest.

Preheat the oven to 400°F (204°C).

Make the pear filling. In a large bowl, stir together the pears, granulated sugar, lemon juice, vanilla, flour, cinnamon, and salt.

On a lightly floured work surface, roll out one disk of the dough to create an 11½-inch (29-cm) circle. Fit the dough into a 10-inch (25-cm) pie dish. Roll out the second disk of dough to create an 11-inch (28-cm) circle. Gently press the edible flowers onto the dough. Use a rolling pin, lightly roll over the flowers to secure them. If you are making a lattice top, cut the dough into 1-inch (2.5-cm)-wide strips.

Transfer the pear filling to the pie dish and arrange the slices so there are no gaps. Dot the pears with the butter.

(Continued)

PEAR PIE WITH PRESSED-FLOWER CRUST *(Continued)*

To assemble the lattice, place the longest strip of pie dough down the middle of the filled pie. Place the other strips of pie dough on both sides of the center strip, leaving a 1-inch (2.5-cm) gap between each strip, until you reach the edge of the pie. To create the woven lattice, lift up every other strip on the pie to the halfway mark. Place a new strip of pie dough perpendicular to the pieces already there. Take the pieces that were lifted up and place them over the new perpendicular piece. Repeat these steps with the pieces of dough that are now under the perpendicular piece. Repeat until you reach the edge of the pie and each piece of dough is in an over-under-over pattern. See photos on page 109.

Trim any pie dough hanging over the edges of the pie dish. To make a crimped edge all around the pie, push down and slightly outward from the inside of the pie with your dominant index finger, and let the V shape formed by your thumb and index finger of your nondominant hand form the crimp shape from the outside edge of the dough as you push. Start the next crimp where the first one ended, and work your way around the pie.

In a small bowl, whisk together the egg and water to create an egg wash. Brush the egg wash over the pie and sprinkle it with the coarse sanding sugar.

Place the pie on a large rimmed baking sheet to catch any juices that might bubble over. Bake the pie on the baking sheet for 20 minutes. Reduce the oven's temperature to 350°F (177°C) and bake the pie for 40 to 50 minutes, or until the crust is golden brown and the filling begins to bubble through the lattice or vents. Let the pie cool for about 3 hours on a wire rack.

Garnish the pie with additional edible flowers and serve it warm with ice cream.

SUMMER FRUIT TART

Unfussy yet impressive, this summer fruit tart allows all the summer produce to shine. The rich and buttery crust is filled with a lightly sweetened rose-mascarpone whipped cream and topped with all the best fruits from the farmers' market. When you make the whipped cream, increase the amount of sugar, 1 tablespoon (13 g) at a time, if the fruits are not as ripe as you'd like.

Yields 1 (9-inch [23-cm]) tart

Pâte Sablée
9 tbsp (126 g) unsalted butter, at room temperature

1/3 cup (40 g) powdered sugar

1 large egg yolk

1¼ cups (150 g) all-purpose flour

1/2 tsp salt

Rose-Mascarpone Whipped Cream
1½ cups (360 ml) heavy cream

1/2 tsp culinary-grade rose water

1/3 cup (40 g) powdered sugar

2/3 cup (150 g) mascarpone cheese, at room temperature

Topping
1 cup (144 g) fresh strawberries, halved

1 cup (144 g) fresh blackberries

1 cup (225 g) fresh whole cherries

1/2 cup (75 g) fresh currants

Make the pâte sablée. In the bowl of a stand mixer fitted with a paddle attachment, beat the butter and powdered sugar on medium speed for about 2 minutes, until they are smooth and creamy. Add the egg yolk and mix until the ingredients are fully combined.

With the mixer on low speed, add the flour and salt and mix just until the dough comes together and there is no more visible flour, about 1 minute. (Be careful not to overmix.) Press the dough into a 9-inch (23-cm) nonstick tart pan with a removable bottom, making sure it is evenly distributed. Using a fork, prick the bottom of the tart crust to prevent the bottom from puffing up during baking. Loosely wrap the tart pan in plastic and chill it in the refrigerator for 30 minutes.

While the tart crust is chilling, preheat the oven to 410°F (210°C).

Remove the tart crust from the refrigerator and immediately place it in the oven. Bake the tart crust for 12 to 15 minutes, until it is golden brown. Carefully remove the tart crust from the oven and let it cool completely on a wire rack.

Make the rose-mascarpone whipped cream. In the bowl of a stand mixer fitted with a whisk attachment, whisk the heavy cream on high speed for about 2 minutes, until medium-stiff peaks form. Reduce the mixer's speed to medium and add the rose water and powdered sugar. Whisk until the ingredients are combined, about 30 seconds. Transfer the whipped cream to a large bowl and set aside.

In the same bowl of the stand mixer fitted with a paddle attachment, beat the mascarpone on high speed for about 2 minutes, until it is smooth and fluffy. With a rubber spatula, gently fold the whipped cream into the mascarpone until the two are incorporated. Transfer the whipped cream to the refrigerator until you are ready to use it.

To assemble the tart, fill the cooled tart crust with the rose-mascarpone whipped cream and top it with the strawberries, blackberries, cherries, and currants.

STRAWBERRY, RHUBARB, *and* ROSE FRANGIPANE TART

This is the dessert I make the most in the summertime. No other dessert even comes close to this one. Friends often ask me, "What is frangipane like?" I like to describe it this way: "It's as if you're eating the filling of a double-baked almond croissant." At this point, their eyes will widen with excitement. There are four components to this tart—a buttery and rich tart crust; a sweet and tangy layer of strawberry, rhubarb, and rose compote; the most luscious almond frangipane filling; and roasted rhubarb. This tart is great when served as is, but it's even better when served warm with a scoop of vanilla ice cream.

Yields 1 (9-inch [23-cm]) tart

Strawberry, Rhubarb, and Rose Compote

1 tbsp (14 g) unsalted butter

1 cup (100 g) trimmed and coarsely chopped rhubarb

1 cup (144 g) fresh strawberries, hulled and coarsely chopped

1/3 cup (67 g) granulated sugar

2 tsp (10 ml) pure vanilla extract

1/2 tsp rose water

Pâte Sablée

9 tbsp (126 g) unsalted butter, at room temperature

1/3 cup (40 g) powdered sugar

1 large egg yolk

1¼ cups (150 g) all-purpose flour

1/2 tsp salt

Make the strawberry, rhubarb, and rose compote. In a heavy medium saucepan over medium heat, melt the butter. Add the rhubarb, strawberries, granulated sugar, vanilla, and rose water. Allow the mixture to cook, undisturbed, for 2 minutes. Gently stir and continue to cook for 10 to 15 minutes, stirring occasionally, until the rhubarb is tender and the juices have become thick. Remove the saucepan from the heat and let the compote cool as you make the tart crust. (This will make a bit more compote than you will need for the tart.)

Make the pâte sablée. In the bowl of a stand mixer fitted with a paddle attachment, beat together the butter and powdered sugar on medium speed until they are creamy, about 1 minute. Add the egg yolk and mix until the ingredients are fully combined. With the mixer on low speed, add the flour and salt and beat just until the dough comes together and there is no more visible flour, about 1 minute. (Be careful not to overmix.) Press the dough into a 9-inch (23-cm) nonstick tart pan with a removable bottom, making sure it is evenly distributed. Using a fork, prick the bottom of the tart crust to prevent the bottom from puffing up during baking. Loosely wrap the tart pan in plastic and chill it in the refrigerator for 30 minutes.

While the tart crust is chilling, preheat the oven to 350°F (177°C).

Bake the tart crust for 10 to 12 minutes, until the crust is light gold in color. The crust should not be too brown, because the tart will be baked again once it has been filled with frangipane. Remove the tart crust from the oven and let it cool on a wire rack for 10 to 15 minutes. Do not turn off the oven.

(Continued)

STRAWBERRY, RHUBARB, AND ROSE FRANGIPANE TART
(Continued)

Roasted Rhubarb

5 to 6 (8- to 10-inch [20- to 25-cm]-long ribs rhubarb, trimmed

⅓ cup (67 g) granulated sugar

1 tsp pure vanilla extract

Almond Frangipane Filling

1¼ cups (125 g) ground almonds

¼ cup (30 g) all-purpose flour

1 tsp baking powder

½ tsp salt

¾ cup (150 g) granulated sugar

⅔ cup (150 g) unsalted butter, at room temperature

2 large eggs, at room temperature

1 tsp pure vanilla extract

Make the roasted rhubarb. Line a large rimmed baking sheet with parchment paper. Place the rhubarb on the prepared baking sheet in a single layer. Evenly sprinkle the rhubarb with the sugar and vanilla. Roast the rhubarb for 15 to 20 minutes, or until it is tender. Do not turn off the oven.

Make the almond frangipane filling. In a medium bowl, whisk together the almonds, flour, baking powder, and salt. Set the almond mixture aside.

In the bowl of a stand mixer fitted with a paddle attachment, combine the granulated sugar and butter. Beat the sugar and butter on medium speed until the mixture is creamy, about 1 minute. With the mixer still running, add the eggs, one at a time, and mix until they are incorporated. Mix in the vanilla. Add the almond mixture and mix until it is just combined and no streaks of dry ingredients remain.

To assemble the tart, spread about ½ cup (163 g) of the strawberry, rhubarb, and rose compote onto the tart crust. Fill the crust with the almond frangipane filling and smooth the top with a spatula or the back of a spoon. Arrange the roasted rhubarb on top of the frangipane.

Bake the tart for 40 to 45 minutes, until the top of the frangipane is golden. Let the tart cool in the pan for 15 minutes before removing it.

HIBISCUS-GLAZED APPLE-PISTACHIO FRANGIPANE TART

I like to make my Strawberry, Rhubarb, and Rose Frangipane Tart (page 112) in the summer, but then I slowly transition to apple frangipane tarts in the fall. This frangipane filling is a mixture of both almonds and pistachios, but you can easily replace the pistachio meal with the same amount of almond flour if you do not have pistachio meal handy. Having something fruity and acidic balances out the richness of frangipane, and both the tart apples and hibiscus-lemon glaze add just that.

Yields 1 (9-inch [23-cm]) tart

Pâte Sablée

9 tbsp (126 g) unsalted butter, at room temperature

1/3 cup (40 g) powdered sugar

1 large egg yolk

1 1/4 cups (150 g) all-purpose flour

1/2 tsp salt

Almond-Pistachio Frangipane Filling

3/4 cup (75 g) almond flour

1/2 cup (50 g) pistachio meal

1/4 cup (30 g) all-purpose flour

1 tsp baking powder

1/2 tsp salt

3/4 cup (150 g) granulated sugar

2/3 cup (150 g) unsalted butter, at room temperature

2 large eggs, at room temperature

1 tsp pure vanilla extract

Make the pâte sablée. In the bowl of a stand mixer fitted with a paddle attachment, beat together the butter and powdered sugar on medium speed until they are creamy, about 1 minute. Beat in the egg yolk and mix until the ingredients are fully combined. With the mixer on low speed, beat in the flour and salt just until the dough comes together and there is no more visible flour, about 1 minute. Press the dough into a 9-inch (23-cm) nonstick tart pan with a removable bottom, making sure it is evenly distributed. Using a fork, prick the bottom of the tart crust to prevent the bottom from puffing up during baking. Loosely wrap the tart pan in plastic and chill it in the refrigerator for at least 30 minutes.

Preheat the oven to 350°F (177°C). Bake the tart crust for about 10 minutes, until the crust is a light gold color. You do not want the crust to be too brown, as it will be baked again after filling. Let the tart crust cool for 10 to 15 minutes on a wire rack.

Make the almond-pistachio frangipane filling. In a medium bowl, whisk together the almond flour, pistachio meal, all-purpose flour, baking powder, and salt. Set the mixture aside.

In the bowl of a stand mixer fitted with a paddle attachment, beat together the granulated sugar and butter on medium speed until they are creamy, about 1 minute. Add the eggs, one at a time, and mix until they are well incorporated. Add the vanilla. With the mixer on low, slowly incorporate the almond flour mixture. Continue mixing on low for 1 to 2 minutes, until no streaks of dry ingredients remain.

Transfer the frangipane filling to the cooled tart crust and even out the filling with an offset spatula or the back of a spoon.

(Continued)

HIBISCUS-GLAZED APPLE-PISTACHIO FRANGIPANE TART
(Continued)

Apple Layer
4 to 5 medium tart apples, peeled, cored, and sliced ¼ inch (6 mm) thick

Hibiscus-Lemon Glaze
½ cup (120 ml) fresh lemon juice

½ cup (100 g) granulated sugar

¼ cup (60 ml) water

½ cup (20 g) dried culinary-grade hibiscus flowers or 4 bags hibiscus tea

Make the apple layer. Fan the apple slices on top of the frangipane filling in a circular pattern until the filling is completely covered.

Bake the tart for 35 to 40 minutes, rotating it halfway through the baking time, until the crust is a deep golden brown. If the apples are browning too quickly, place a piece of aluminum foil loosely on top of the tart. Allow the tart to cool inside the tart pan on a wire rack.

Make the hibiscus-lemon glaze. In a small saucepan over medium-high heat, combine the lemon juice, granulated sugar, and water. Bring the mixture just to a boil. Add the hibiscus flowers. Reduce the heat to medium-low to maintain a gentle simmer and cook until the syrup is slightly thickened, about 10 minutes. Strain the mixture through a fine-mesh sieve to remove the flowers. Set the glaze aside to cool.

Once the glaze has cooled, use a pastry brush to brush a thin layer of the hibiscus-lemon glaze on top of the tart.

NO-BAKE HONEY BLOSSOM CHEESECAKE TART *with* PLUMS

I love no-bake desserts any time of the year. They come together quickly, and I have always had an undying love for any dessert with a tender unbaked graham crust. The filling of this tart is an airy and velvety cheesecake filling flavored with orange blossom water. Fluffy whipped cream is gently folded into cream cheese to create a light filling that still has the richness we associate with a traditional cheesecake. I top this tart with plums tossed in a bit of honey for extra shine, but you can top it with any fruit of your choice.

Yields 1 (9- to 10-inch [23- to 25-cm]) tart

Graham Tart Crust
1½ cups (128 g) graham cracker crumbs

5 tbsp (70 g) unsalted butter, melted

⅓ cup (67 g) granulated sugar

No-Bake Cheesecake Filling
1½ cups (360 ml) heavy cream

1 cup (224 g) cream cheese, at room temperature

½ cup (60 g) powdered sugar

¾ tsp culinary-grade orange blossom water

½ tsp pure vanilla extract

½ tsp salt

Topping
6 to 7 medium plums, cut into ¼-inch (6-mm)-thick slices

1 tbsp (15 ml) honey

Make the graham tart crust. In a medium bowl, mix together the graham cracker crumbs, butter, and granulated sugar with a rubber spatula until the ingredients are combined. The mixture should resemble wet sand. Press the mixture into the bottom and up the sides of a 9- to 10-inch (23- to 25-cm) nonstick tart pan with a removable bottom. Use the bottom of a flat measuring cup or your hand to press down on the graham mixture to form a tight and compact crust. Cover the crust loosely with plastic wrap and chill the crust in the freezer as you make the filling.

Make the no-bake cheesecake filling. Pour the heavy cream into the bowl of a stand mixer fitted with a whisk attachment. Whisk the heavy cream on high speed for 2 to 3 minutes, until it becomes fluffy and forms medium-stiff peaks. Transfer the whipped cream into a large bowl.

Secure the paddle attachment to the stand mixer and beat the cream cheese on high speed for about 2 minutes, until it is light and fluffy. Add the powdered sugar, orange blossom water, vanilla, and salt and beat on medium-high for 2 to 3 minutes, until it is light and fluffy. Transfer the whipped cream to the mixer bowl and gently fold it into the cream cheese mixture with a rubber spatula.

Remove the chilled crust from the freezer. Fill the tart with the cheesecake filling and smooth it out with the back of a spoon or an offset spatula. Cover the tart loosely in plastic wrap and refrigerate it for at least 3 hours or overnight.

When you are ready to serve the tart, make the topping. In a medium bowl, toss the plums with the honey. Using a slotted spoon, transfer the plums to the top of the tart without transferring any of their liquid.

APPLE-ROSE CUSTARD TART

Every year, at the beginning of apple season, I make an apple-rose custard tart. I dedicate an entire afternoon to making apple roses that I arrange on a luscious custard inside a buttery tart crust. Using a variety of apples means that each apple rose is a different color and size. The key to making perfect apple roses is to slice the apples very thin—having a mandoline can be quite helpful. Thicker slices of apples can be hard to bend and might end up snapping when bent to form a rose petal.

Yields 1 (9-inch [23-cm]) tart

Pâte Sablée

9 tbsp (126 g) unsalted butter, at room temperature

1/3 cup (40 g) powdered sugar

1 large egg yolk

1¼ cups (150 g) all-purpose flour

1/2 tsp salt

Vanilla Custard

1 cup (240 ml) whole milk

1 cup (240 ml) heavy cream

4 bags jasmine green tea

Seeds of 1 vanilla bean

4 large egg yolks

1 tbsp (8 g) cornstarch

1/2 cup (100 g) granulated sugar

Preheat the oven to 410°F (210°C).

Make the pâte sablée. In the bowl of a stand mixer fitted with a paddle attachment, beat together the butter and powdered sugar on medium speed until they are creamy, about 1 minute. Beat in the egg yolk and mix until the ingredients are fully combined.

With the mixer on low speed, mix in the flour and salt until the dough comes together and there is no more visible flour, about 1 minute. Be careful not to overmix the dough. Press the dough into a 9-inch (23-cm) nonstick tart pan with a removable bottom, making sure it is evenly distributed. Using a fork, prick the bottom of the tart crust to prevent the bottom from puffing up during baking. Loosely wrap the tart pan in plastic and chill it in the refrigerator for at least 30 minutes.

Bake the tart crust for 12 to 15 minutes, until it is golden. Remove the tart crust from the oven and let it cool completely on a wire rack.

Make the vanilla custard. In a small saucepan, combine the milk, heavy cream, tea bags, and seeds of the vanilla bean. Place the mixture over medium heat. Cook for 5 minutes, stirring constantly, or until the mixture is hot (do not allow it to boil). Remove the saucepan from the heat and remove the tea bags.

In a medium bowl, whisk together the egg yolks, cornstarch, and granulated sugar. Slowly pour the hot milk mixture over the egg yolk mixture, whisking constantly.

Return the mixture to the saucepan over low heat. Cook, stirring constantly, for 10 to 15 minutes, or until the custard thickens and coats the back of a spoon. Remove the custard from the heat and transfer it to a medium bowl. Cover the bowl in plastic wrap and chill the custard in the refrigerator for at least 2 hours, until it is no longer hot.

(Continued)

APPLE-ROSE CUSTARD TART *(Continued)*

Apple Roses

½ cup (120 ml) fresh orange juice

½ cup (100 g) granulated sugar

2 tbsp (28 g) unsalted butter

5 to 6 large apples (see note)

Make the apple roses. In a medium pot over medium heat, combine the orange juice, granulated sugar, and butter. Remove the mixture from the heat once it starts to boil.

Peel and core the apples, then cut them in half. Using a very sharp knife or a mandoline, slice the apples paper thin, about ⅛ inch (3 mm) thick.

Place the sliced apples in the orange juice mixture. Cover the pot with its lid. Soak the apples for 15 minutes, until they are pliable.

Remove the apple slices from the liquid and transfer them to a large plate. Pat them with a paper towel.

To form an apple rose, use the smaller apple slices to overlap the ends of each slice so that you have a row of connected half ovals. Roll up the row of apple slices so that both ends of the row overlap a little; this will form the center of the rose. Take a slightly larger apple slice and wrap it around the center of the rose. Continue until you have a fully "bloomed" apple rose.

Fill the tart crust with the chilled custard. Arrange the apple roses on top of the custard.

Note: I generally use a mix of Ambrosia, Pink Lady, and Fuji apples, so there's more variation in color and flavor.

JASMINE FRUIT TARTLETS

These tartlets are inspired by my favorite after-school treat I ate growing up—mini fruit tartlets from the local Chinese bakery. These tartlets consisted of fresh fruit, custard, and a buttery tart crust. I still buy these fruit tarts from time to time, but I also like making my grown-up version. The base of these tarts is a pâte sablée, a crisp and cookie-like crust that crumbles a bit but is far from dry. It is filled with a delicate whipped white chocolate ganache infused with jasmine green tea and topped with fresh fruit. I like to use whatever fruit is in season, but strawberries and peaches will always be my preference.

Yields 10 to 12 tartlets

Whipped Jasmine Green Tea Ganache
2/3 cup (117 g) coarsely chopped white chocolate

1 cup (240 ml) heavy cream

5 bags jasmine green tea

1/2 tsp salt

Pâte Sablée
9 tbsp (126 g) unsalted butter, at room temperature, plus more as needed

1/3 cup (40 g) powdered sugar

1 large egg yolk

1¼ cups (150 g) all-purpose flour

1/2 tsp salt

Garnish
Assorted fresh fruit, as needed

Make the whipped jasmine green tea ganache. Place the white chocolate into a medium heatproof bowl.

In a small pot over medium heat, bring the heavy cream to a boil. Remove the pot from the heat and place the bags of jasmine green tea in the cream. Place a lid on the pot and allow the tea to steep in the cream for 20 minutes. Pour the cream over the chocolate and let the mixture sit for 1 minute. Add the salt and whisk the chocolate mixture until the chocolate has thoroughly melted and is combined with the cream. Cover the bowl with plastic wrap and set it in the refrigerator to chill at least 4 hours.

Make the pâte sablée. In the bowl of a stand mixer fitted with a paddle attachment, beat together the butter and powdered sugar at medium speed until they are creamy, about 1 minute. Beat in the egg yolk and mix until the ingredients are fully combined. With the mixer on low speed, beat in the flour and salt, just until the dough comes together and there is no more visible flour, about 1 minute. Be careful not to overmix the dough.

Grease 10 to 12 mini tart pans with the additional butter. Press about 2 tablespoons (20 g) of dough into each tart pan, making sure it is evenly distributed. Using a fork, prick the bottoms of the tart crusts to prevent the bottoms from puffing up during baking. Place the tart pans on a small baking sheet. Loosely wrap the baking sheet in plastic and chill the tart crusts in the refrigerator for 30 minutes.

Preheat the oven to 350°F (177°C). Bake the tart crusts for 14 to 16 minutes, until the crusts are golden. Remove the tart crusts from the oven and let them cool completely on a wire rack.

Once the tart crusts have cooled and the ganache is chilled, transfer the ganache to the bowl of a stand mixer fitted with a whisk attachment. Whisk the ganache on high speed for 2 to 3 minutes, until the ganache is fluffy. Transfer the whipped ganache to a piping bag fitted with a large round pastry tip and pipe it into the tart crusts. Garnish the tartlets with the fruit.

Other Floral Treats

Just because some treats do not fall into the categories of cake, cookies, choux, or pie does not mean they deserve less love. Rose Blossom Mochi (page 129) and Jasmine Mooncakes (page 132) are inspired by Asian treats I ate growing up, and Floral Caramels (page 135) and Rose Lollipops (page 136) are more elegant and romantic versions of candies I loved during my childhood. Lastly, No-Churn Rose-Pistachio Ice Cream Sandwiches (page 130) can be enjoyed even on days when you forgot to chill your ice cream maker the night before.

ROSE BLOSSOM MOCHI

Growing up in an Asian household meant I ate many forms of mochi. I would have homemade mochi made by my mom, mochi balls at dim sum, and store-bought mochi filled with fruit or bean paste. Generally, I like mochi more than the filling it surrounds—when my mom made mochi, I always requested for them to be plain. These rose blossom mochi flowers are a combination of what I loved in the past and what I love now. Sweetened baked mochi is lightly scented with rose water (or any other floral flavors of your choice) and cut into little cherry blossoms.

Yields 1 (9 x 13-inch [23 x 33-cm]) pan

1¼ cups (190 g) sweet rice flour (mochiko)

1 cup (200 g) granulated sugar

½ tsp baking powder

1¼ cups (300 ml) full-fat coconut milk

1 cup (240 ml) water

½ tsp culinary-grade rose water

Toasted rice flour, as needed

Preheat the oven to 275°F (135°C). Generously grease a 9 x 13-inch (23 x 33-cm) baking pan and line it with parchment paper, leaving overhang on at least two sides of the pan.

In a medium bowl, whisk together the sweet rice flour, sugar, and baking powder.

Add the coconut milk, water, and rose water to the bowl, whisking to combine. Strain the mixture through a fine-mesh sieve to remove any clumps.

Transfer the mochi mixture to the baking pan. Tightly cover the baking pan with aluminum foil and bake the mochi for 60 to 70 minutes, until the mochi has set. Allow the mochi to cool completely before removing it from the baking pan.

Gently sprinkle the toasted rice flour on the surface of the mochi to prevent the surface from sticking to your knife or cookie cutter. Cut the mochi into squares or punch out shapes with your favorite flower-shaped cookie cutter.

Note: If using a cookie cutter to cut out shapes, punch the cutouts close together because leftover mochi cannot be gathered and rolled out again.

NO-CHURN ROSE-PISTACHIO ICE CREAM SANDWICHES

There are times for ice cream made with a custard base that's cooked over the stove and churned in an ice cream maker, but there are also times for a simple no-churn ice cream that comes together with few ingredients and tools. In this recipe, a simple no-churn rose ice cream studded with raspberries and pistachios is sandwiched between two cookies of your choice. I like using less-sweet and simpler cookies like speculoos cookies or sugar cookies to sandwich the ice cream.

Yields 10 to 12 ice cream sandwiches

9 oz (266 ml) sweetened condensed milk

1 tsp pure vanilla extract

½ tsp culinary-grade rose water

¼ tsp salt

2 cups (480 ml) heavy cream

1½ cups (160 g) fresh raspberries, divided

½ cup (60 g) roasted pistachios, coarsely chopped

20 to 24 cookies of choice

Line a 9 x 13-inch (23 x 33-cm) baking pan with parchment paper, leaving some parchment paper hanging over both sides. Set the baking pan aside.

In a large bowl, combine the condensed milk, vanilla, rose water, and salt. Set the milk mixture aside.

In the bowl of a stand mixer fitted with a whisk attachment, whisk the heavy cream on high speed for 2 to 3 minutes, until medium-stiff peaks form.

Fold about 1 cup (60 g) of the whipped cream into the condensed milk mixture to lighten the milk mixture. Then fold in the remaining whipped cream.

In a small bowl, mash ¾ cup (80 g) of the raspberries with a fork. Fold the mashed raspberries and their juices, the remaining ¾ cup (80 g) of raspberries, and the pistachios into the ice cream mixture.

Transfer the ice cream mixture into the prepared baking pan and cover the pan tightly with plastic wrap. Freeze the ice cream for 4 to 5 hours (or preferably overnight) until it is firm.

Lift the ice cream from the baking pan and use a large knife or cookie cutter to cut out 10 to 12 portions roughly the same size as the cookies you are using. To assemble the ice cream cookies, top a cookie with the ice cream, then place another cookie on top. Serve immediately.

JASMINE MOONCAKES

Every year my family would celebrate Mid-Autumn Festival (which is like a Chinese Thanksgiving to celebrate harvest and family) with a large family dinner and, of course, mooncakes. There are two types of mooncakes: traditional baked mooncakes and "snowy" mooncakes that have a mochi-like exterior. These are the latter, and they are filled with a thick jasmine custard.

Yields 8 to 10 mooncakes

Snowy Mooncake Wrapper
3/4 cup (180 ml) plus 2 tbsp (30 ml) unsweetened full-fat coconut milk

1 tbsp (15 ml) vegetable oil

1/3 cup (40 g) plus 1 tbsp (8 g) powdered sugar

1/3 cup (50 g) glutinous rice flour

3 1/2 tbsp (35 g) rice flour

2 tbsp (20 g) tapioca flour

Jasmine Custard Filling
2 tbsp (24 g) custard powder

1/2 cup (60 g) wheat starch

1 tbsp (5 g) all-purpose flour

3/4 cup (180 ml) whole milk, divided

2 large eggs

1/2 cup (100 g) granulated sugar

2 tbsp (28 g) unsalted butter

Toasted rice flour, as needed

Make the snowy mooncake wrapper. Combine the coconut milk and oil in a large measuring cup.

In a medium bowl, whisk together the powdered sugar, glutinous rice flour, rice flour, and tapioca flour.

Pour the coconut milk mixture into the powdered sugar mixture and mix well using a whisk, making sure no clumps remain. Strain the mixture through a fine-meshed sieve to remove any clumps. Use the back of a spoon to press out any remaining clumps.

Place the bowl in the steamer insert of a large pot of water over medium heat. Steam the mixture in the bowl for 30 minutes, until it becomes slightly transparent. Remove the bowl from the pot and stir the mixture with chopsticks for about 2 minutes, until the mixture is glossy and smooth. Transfer the dough to a plate and cover it with plastic wrap. Knead the dough for 3 to 4 minutes, until the surface becomes glossy and oily. Form the dough into a disk and refrigerate it for at least 3 hours before assembling the mooncakes. (A warm dough is too sticky to handle.)

Make the jasmine custard filling. In a medium bowl, whisk together the custard powder, wheat starch, and all-purpose flour. Add 1/2 cup (120 ml) of the milk to the mixture and mix until no clumps remain. Set this mixture aside.

In a medium bowl, whisk the eggs. Set the eggs aside.

In a small pot over low heat, dissolve the granulated sugar with the remaining ¼ cup (60 ml) of milk. Once the mixture starts to simmer, remove it from the heat. While whisking constantly, slowly stream the hot milk mixture into the eggs. Whisk until the ingredients are combined. Return the mixture to the pot over low heat. Add the custard powder mixture, stirring to combine. Add the butter. Keep stirring to prevent the mixture from clumping. Heat the mixture until it becomes thick and forms a paste, about 3 to 4 minutes (the texture will change quickly). Remove the pot from the heat and keep stirring the custard for 1 to 2 minutes, until it is smooth. Transfer the custard paste to a medium bowl. Tightly cover the bowl with plastic wrap. Refrigerate the custard for at least 2 hours, until it is firm and you can shape it easily.

To assemble the mooncakes, using a 1¾-ounce (50-g) mooncake press, weigh out 1¼-ounce (35-g) scoops of the custard filling and gently shape each portion into balls. Set the balls aside.

Divide and weigh the dough into 0.5-ounce (15-g) pieces. Roll out each piece of dough between two pieces of plastic wrap until they are ⅛ inch (3 mm) thick.

Place a ball of filling in the center of each piece of dough. Wrap the filling with the rolled-out wrapper dough and seal the filling completely in the dough. Shape the mooncake into an oval shape, so it will easily slide into the mooncake mold. Dust the mooncake mold with toasted rice flour and insert the dough ball into the press. Press on the mooncake mold to shape the mooncake. Carefully remove the mooncake from the press. If any part of the mooncake is too tacky, brush on more toasted rice flour.

*See photo on page 126.

FLORAL CARAMELS

These are not the hard square caramels in the neatly folded clear wrappers. Instead, they are soft and creamy with the right amount of chew. They also have a good amount of salt, both in the caramel candy and on top, because caramel just calls for salt. These salted caramels are the perfect canvas for any floral flavor. Add your favorite flower waters or extracts to the caramel as it cooks, starting with ¼ teaspoon, to give an elegant twist to this classic confection.

Yields 1 (8 x 8-inch [20 x 20-cm]) pan of caramels

1⅓ cups (320 ml) heavy cream

1¼ cups (250 g) granulated sugar

¼ cup (50 g) packed brown sugar

⅓ cup (80 ml) light corn syrup

1 tsp salt

2 tsp (10 ml) pure vanilla extract

¼ tsp jasmine extract or floral extract of choice

2 tbsp (28 g) unsalted butter, at room temperature

Flaky sea salt, as needed

Line an 8 x 8-inch (20 x 20-cm) square baking pan with parchment paper, leaving enough overhang on the sides to easily remove the caramel once it has set. Lightly grease the parchment with butter.

In a large heavy-bottomed saucepan over medium heat, combine the heavy cream, granulated sugar, brown sugar, and corn syrup. Using a wooden spoon, stir constantly as the sugars dissolve. The mixture will be thick and cloudy. Attach a candy thermometer to the saucepan, making sure not to let it touch the bottom.

Cook and stir the mixture gently every 60 seconds, until the temperature reaches 245°F (118°C) on the thermometer. Remove the saucepan from the heat and stir in the salt, vanilla, jasmine extract, and butter. The mixture will bubble, so be careful when stirring.

Pour the hot caramel into the prepared baking pan and top it with the flaky sea salt. Allow the caramel to cool at room temperature, uncovered, for at least 4 hours or overnight. Once it has set, remove the caramel from the pan by lifting the overhang of parchment paper. Peel the paper off of the caramel and, using a very sharp knife, cut it into rectangles or squares.

 Note: For thicker pieces of caramel, use a standard load pan instead of a square 8 x 8-inch (20 x 20-cm) pan.

ROSE LOLLIPOPS

These lollipops are the grown-up version of the brightly colored lollipops reminiscent of childhood. They make great homemade gifts during the holidays because they stay fresher for a longer period of time compared to traditional baked goods. This is a great "blank canvas" recipe—feel free to sub any other flavorings you like for the rose water. I like to flavor these lollipops with rose water and add rose petals and edible gold leaf during the holidays for a festive look, but I often swap those elements for brighter and fruitier flavors during the spring and summer.

Yields 24 (1-inch [2.5-cm]) lollipops

1 cup (200 g) granulated sugar

½ cup (120 ml) water

¼ cup (60 ml) corn syrup

½ tsp culinary-grade rose water

Gel food coloring (optional)

Dried culinary-grade rose petals, crushed, as needed

Edible gold leaf, as needed

In a large saucepan over medium heat, combine the sugar, water, and corn syrup. Attach a candy thermometer to the saucepan, making sure not to let it touch the bottom. Bring the mixture to a boil. Cook until the mixture reaches 300°F (149°C), or hard-crack stage, as detected by the candy thermometer. Immediately remove the saucepan from the heat. Stir in the rose water. Stir in the food coloring (if using).

Spray the lollipop molds lightly with nonstick cooking spray. Place the rose petals and gold leaf into each lollipop cavity. Fill each cavity halfway with the sugar mixture, insert a lollipop stick, and fill the remaining half of the cavity. Let the lollipops cool and harden for 25 to 30 minutes before removing them from the molds.

Decoration Tutorials and Techniques

I love decorating as much as I love baking, if not even more. Throughout this book, a lot of the recipes covered decorating elements, like the Lilac-Vanilla Cupcakes (page 49), the "Flowerfetti" Brown Butter Apple Cake with Cream Cheese Buttercream (page 33), and the Pear Pie with Pressed-Flower Crust (page 107). But in this chapter, we are going to go into more detail on ways to add floral decorations. We will first talk about how to create the most romantic and rustic naked cake with fresh flowers. Then we will learn about piping tips and learn how to pipe your favorite flowers, which you can use to top any cupcakes or the One-Bowl Chocolate Sheet Cake with Buttercream Flowers (page 29). Lastly, we will assemble an impressive cookie box, which makes the perfect holiday gift, with most of the cookies from the chapter on cookies.

DECORATING WITH FRESH FLOWERS

My favorite way to decorate any cake or tart is to decorate with fresh flowers—they bring so much life to a cake and a certain type of elegance that cannot be replicated. Like baking with flowers, there are some things one should consider before decorating with flowers.

Decorating with Inedible Flowers

When you are decorating with inedible flowers, organic flowers are preferred. You do not want to put flowers that have been treated with chemicals on top of a cake that is going to be consumed. I ask my favorite florist about the treatment of flowers I want to use for my cakes. She has great knowledge of which organic flowers are in season and can make wonderful suggestions.

If there is a certain type of flower I want to decorate with, but I do not know whether it is organic, I like to wash and prep the stems thoroughly. Trim the stems to the desired length and wash them under cold water. While running them under cold water, use your fingers to brush the exterior petals that will be in contact with the cake. After washing the flowers, dry them immediately with paper towels. After the flowers have dried, wrap plastic wrap or green floral tape around the stems before placing them onto or into the cake.

Decorate the cake with flowers no earlier than 24 hours before serving. I prefer to decorate the cake just a few hours before serving.

Obviously, do not decorate your cake with poisonous flowers!

Decorating with Edible Flowers

You can plant and grow your own edible flowers; however, I find it most convenient to purchase them at the farmers' market or my local Whole Foods. You can also buy fresh edible flowers online! Keep in mind that online shops will ship the flowers directly to you via Priority Mail, so the shipping costs may be expensive.

Some of my favorite edible flowers include pansies, violas, roses, and chamomile. Though they are beautiful, I would avoid using edible flowers like chive blossoms, which may impart an onion-like taste to your baked goods.

NAKED CAKE DECORATING 101

The first cake I ever decorated was a naked cake, and the majority of the cakes I make are naked cakes. I love the way the layers peek from behind the patchwork of buttercream, giving the slightest hint of the flavors of the cake underneath. Naked cakes are rustic and romantic, and they are especially so when adorned with fresh flowers. There are two types of naked cakes: "semi-naked" cakes and true naked cakes. A semi-naked cake (like the pink cake and the white cake in the photo on page 143) has a minimal amount of frosting swiped around the sides, while the sides of a true naked cake are completely bare (like the chocolate cake in the photo on page 143). Whether you are achieving the look of the former or the latter, here are some tips for making the perfect naked cake for any occasion.

Things to Consider before Baking the Cake

- Naked cakes have less frosting to hold the cake together compared to a fully frosted cake, so steer away from choosing a cake with an extremely delicate crumb. If you do choose a more delicate cake, remember to handle it gently, especially when taking the cake out of the pan and transferring it to the cake stand.

- The sides of the cake are going to be visible because there will only be a thin layer of frosting (if any) on the sides, so any large tears or chunks missing will be noticeable. To ensure your cakes come out of the cake pans nicely, grease the cake pans well and use parchment paper to line the bottoms of the pans. If your cake does get stuck or there is a small chunk missing, just give that spot a little extra love and care in the form of buttercream.

- Choose a sturdier buttercream for naked cakes. American buttercream works really well and so does Swiss meringue buttercream. Softer creams, like whipped cream, will hold the cake together but will soften as the cake sits at room temperature for a period of time.

Things to Consider after Baking the Cake

- Just as you would when frosting any other cakes or cupcakes, allow the cake layers to cool completely before assembling the cake. Two things can happen when dealing with a cake that is still warm: the cake will have a much higher chance of crumbling when you trim it and the buttercream will melt when it is applied to a warm cake.

- Use a sharp serrated knife or a cake leveling tool and a steady hand when cutting off rounded tips. Because naked cakes are bare (or nearly bare), it is more obvious when a cake is slanted.

Things to Consider When Assembling the Cake

- Use an ice cream scoop to portion out the frosting for each layer. This ensures equal amounts of frosting between each cake layer so the cake will look particularly beautiful and clean when it is sliced.

- If the cake layers are not equal in thickness, use the thickest or heaviest layer for the bottom. A heavy top layer can weigh down the other layers, causing the buttercream to squish out from the sides.

- Use an offset spatula and bench scraper to smooth out any lumps and bumps. Offset spatulas and bench scrapers are very affordable and will make any cake decorating project much easier.

- Naked cakes are great canvases for decorating. Decorate them with fresh flowers, fruits, macarons—anything, really! For a tutorial on how to prep flowers for decorating cakes, refer to page 140. You can stick to just one type of flower for the cake or use an assortment of colors and types. Sometimes I will use just greenery.

Things to Consider When Storing the Cake

- Take care when storing naked cakes. Since naked cakes have less frosting on the sides to seal in the moisture of the cakes, store them in a cake dome or an airtight container to prevent the cake from drying out.

MAKING CANDIED AND PRESSED PETALS FOR DECORATION

In addition to using fresh flowers and edible flowers for garnish and decoration, candied petals and pressed petals can add an elegant touch to any pastry. Whether you source your petals from your garden or from the market, just be certain they're free of pesticides and other chemicals.

Candied Petals

Sugaring petals gives an extra sparkle to them. It also leaves the petals sweet and crunchy, adding texture to any baked good. Generally, sugaring individual petals is more ideal than sugaring a whole flower, unless the flower is quite small and thin (like pansies and violas). Following are instructions for sugaring petals.

What you will need:

- Egg white
- Granulated sugar

Carefully pluck the individual petals from the edible bloom. Gently wash the petals, trying not to bruise them. Place the petals on a paper towel and let them dry completely. Once the petals have dried, they are ready to be sugared. Place a wire cooling rack on a baking sheet. Crack an egg and separate the white from the yolk; we will be using only the white. Transfer the egg white to a small bowl and whisk it with a fork. Have granulated sugar ready in a separate shallow bowl or plate. Dip the petal in the egg white, turning to coat both sides and allowing any extra to run off. The thinner the layer of egg white, the better. Place the petal in the bowl of sugar, turning the petal to coat both sides and sprinkling on extra sugar if necessary. The petal should be completely coated with sugar. Allow the sugared petals to dry on a wire cooling rack 2 to 3 hours or overnight until they have hardened. Sugared petals are best used within 2 to 3 days.

Find sugared petals on my Coffee and Milk Chocolate Cream Puffs with Candied Rose Petals (page 85).

Pressed Edible Flowers

Pressing edible flowers is much like pressing other flowers. The key to achieving the best pressed edible flowers for decoration is to press it when they are as fresh as possible. If the flowers have a thick or long stem, trim them as close to the flower as possible before pressing. Some edible flowers naturally lie flat (like pansies, plum blossoms, and chamomile), but other flowers (like roses) are more three-dimensional and harder to lay flat. Flowers like roses can still be flattened whole, but they can also be taken apart and the petals can be pressed individually. Following are instructions for pressing flowers.

What you need:

- 2 pieces of copier paper

- Heavy books

- 2 pieces of wax paper

Arrange the flowers between two pieces of copier paper. Open the middle of a heavy book and slip in 2 pieces of wax paper (this will prevent the moisture from the flowers from seeping through onto the book's pages). Slip the paper with the flowers between the wax paper. Use more books or something heavy to weigh down the book once it is closed. Be sure not to disturb the arrangement of the flowers upon closing the book. If the flowers are quite large, change the blotter sheets every few days. After 1 to 2 weeks, the flowers will be completely dry. When removing the flowers, use a pair of tweezers or very carefully use your fingers, as a completely dry flower is very delicate.

Find pressed edible flowers on my Floral Hand Pies (page 103), "Flowerfetti" Brown Butter Apple Cake with Cream Cheese Buttercream (page 33), Floral Almond Wreath Cookies (page 57), and Plum Blossom "Window" Cookies (page 72).

PIPING BUTTERCREAM FLOWERS

My favorite way to decorate baked goods is with fresh flowers, but piped buttercream flowers are a close second. Piped buttercream flowers add a whimsical touch and are especially great for the times a certain flower you want is not in season. There are two things that are important for achieving the perfect buttercream flowers: buttercream consistency and piping tips.

Buttercream Consistency

When piping buttercream flowers, you want a buttercream that is stiffer than softened butter but softer than butter that would be hard to pass through the piping tip. Buttercream that is too stiff can also create unwanted cracks in your buttercream petals. The following is the ratio of ingredients I generally use to make buttercream for piping. I use a mixer to beat the buttercream at medium-high speed for 3 to 4 minutes, until the buttercream is light and airy. If needed, I add more or less milk to reach the desired consistency.

Perfect Vanilla Buttercream for Piping (3½ to 4 cups [980 to 1120 g])

1½ cups (340 g) unsalted butter, at room temperature

4½ to 5½ cups (540 to 660 g) powdered sugar

2 to 4 tbsp (30 to 60 ml) whole milk

2 tsp (10 ml) pure vanilla extract

Pinch of salt

Gel food coloring of choice

Piping Tips

There are many piping tips out there, but for piping buttercream flowers, there are only a few tips that I would consider staples:

- For dahlias or chrysanthemums, use Wilton #81.

- For roses or ruffled peonies, use Wilton #101, #102, #103, #104, or #125 (depending of the size of flower you want to pipe).

- For ranunculus, use Wilton #150.

- For leaves, use Wilton #67, #69, or any leaf tip.

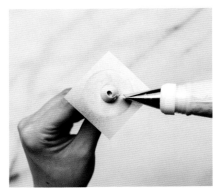

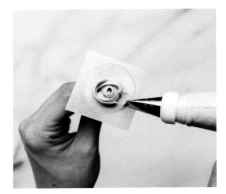

ROSE PIPING TUTORIAL

Piping a rose is how most people get started with buttercream flowers—it is how I got started. The techniques used to pipe a rose can be applied to piping other flowers.

What you need:

- Buttercream, tinted with light pink gel food coloring (page 149)
- Pastry bag
- Wilton #103 or #104 tip

Make the center bud first. To make this center bud, the wide end of the tip should touch the base of the flower nail or cupcake and the narrow end of the tip should point up and angle slightly inward at about 45 degrees. Squeeze the pastry bag and rotate the flower nail or cupcake to form a ribbon of icing. The ribbon should then form a "cone" and the ends will overlap.

For the first three petals around the bud, touch the wide end of the tip to the midpoint of the bud base, with the narrow end of the tip pointing straight up. As you turn the nail, the in-out-in motion of the tip will make a half-circle upright petal. The wide end of the tip must touch the rose base so that the petal will attach. Start again, slightly behind the end of the first petal, and squeeze out the second petal. Repeat this process for the third petal. The last petal should slightly overlap the beginning of the first petal.

For the remaining petals, repeat the preceding steps to create a second ring of petals. The number and length of the petals will increase with each row.

With an offset spatula, transfer the chilled buttercream rose to the top of a cupcake or cookie.

RANUNCULUS PIPING TUTORIAL

Ranunculus are some of my favorite flowers because of the way their petals overlap. Each petal overlaps with the two beside it to form an X shape. Piped ranunculus look best when two different colors are used to create each bloom. The center bud of ranunculus flowers is usually a light green (or a lighter color of its exterior petals), and I like to color my buttercream in a similar way to make the piped ranunculus more realistic.

What you need:

- Buttercream tinted with moss green gel food coloring (page 149)
- Buttercream tinted with pink gel food coloring (page 149)
- 2 pastry bags
- 2 Wilton #150 tips

With the pastry bag filled with green buttercream, start at the center of the flower. With one end of the piping tip touching the flower nail or cupcake at a 45-degree angle, squeeze the buttercream while slowly turning the nail to form a cone of green buttercream. With the green buttercream, pipe the first petal over the cone, forming an arch. Then slightly turn the nail and overlap a second petal over the first, forming an X shape. Continue turning and overlapping petals, slightly tilting the tip outward, until the desired size is achieved.

Switch to the pink buttercream to continue the same technique of overlapping each previous petal to form an X shape. Continue piping with the pink buttercream until the petals reach the edge of the flower nail or cupcake.

RUFFLED PEONY PIPING TUTORIAL

Piping a ruffled peony is much like piping a rose (page 150), although it is easier than piping a rose because it is supposed to have a messy and ruffled look. Instead of straight petals, wiggle the pastry bag a bit to create a petal with curves and waves.

What you need:

- Buttercream tinted with light pink gel food coloring (page 149)

- Pastry bag

- Wilton #103 or #104 tip

The wide end of the tip should touch the base of the flower nail or cupcake and the narrow end of the tip should point up and angle slightly inward at about 45 degrees. Squeeze the bag and rotate the flower nail between your fingers to form a ribbon of icing. The ribbon should then form a "cone" and the ends will overlap.

Touch the wide end of the tip to the midpoint of the bud's base, with the narrow end of the tip pointing straight up. As you turn the nail, move the tip in and out several times. The wide end of the tip must touch the peony base so that the petal will attach. Start again, slightly behind the end of the first petal, and squeeze out the second petal. Repeat these steps for the third petal. The last petal should slightly overlap the beginning of the first petal.

Repeat the preceding steps to create the second ring of petals. The number and length of the petals will increase with each row.

If the flower was piped on a piece of parchment paper on a flower nail instead of directly onto the cupcake, carefully transfer the flower with the parchment paper onto a plate or baking sheet. Place the baking sheet in the refrigerator or freezer until the flower is firm. Then carefully use an offset spatula to transfer the flower to the cake or cookie.

SUNFLOWER PIPING TUTORIAL

Sunflowers are perhaps the easiest flowers to pipe. There is no need to use a petal tip to form delicate curved petals and to build on the center bud. I love piping sunflowers, because it means my cupcakes are topped with both chocolate and vanilla buttercream.

What you need:

- Buttercream tinted with yellow gel food coloring (page 149)
- Chocolate buttercream (page 48)
- 2 pastry bags
- Wilton #18 tip (for center)
- Wilton #352 tip (for petals)

Using a piping bag fitted with a Wilton #18 tip, pipe dollops of chocolate buttercream at the center of the cupcake. These dollops should form a circle.

Switch to a pastry bag fitted with a Wilton #352 tip and pipe yellow buttercream petals around the chocolate dollops, rotating the cupcake until a full ring of petals has been piped. Continue piping rings of petals until the buttercream reaches the edge of the cupcake.

Note: Unlike the previous piping tutorials (e.g. rose, ranunculus, peony), sunflowers are best when piped directly onto a cupcake instead of a flower nail.

CHRYSANTHEMUM PIPING TUTORIAL

Chrysanthemums have a very distinct petal pattern, with each long, sharp petal facing upward. Together, the flower's small petals form a half-sphere. Chrysanthemums come in many different colors: pink, purple, and yellow being the most popular. This piping technique can also be used to pipe buttercream dahlias.

What you need:

- Buttercream tinted with moss green gel food coloring (page 149)
- Buttercream tinted with light purple gel food coloring (page 149)
- 2 pastry bags
- Wilton #67 tip (for leaves)
- Wilton #81 tip (for petals)

Fit the pastry bag filled with moss green buttercream with a Wilton #67 tip for the leaves. Pipe several leaves around the edge of the cupcake.

Fit the pastry bag filled with light purple buttercream with a Wilton #81 tip for the petals. Hold the pastry bag at a 90-degree angle, with the rounded end of the tip pointed toward the outside (like a backward C shape). Pipe a ring of petals around the cupcake. Continue piping a second row and so on until the petals reach the center of the cupcake. Add any additional petals at the center to fill in the flower.

Note: Like buttercream sunflowers, chrysanthemums are best when piped directly onto the cupcake.

INTRODUCTION TO RUSSIAN PIPING TIPS

Russian piping tips are always what I reach for when I do not feel like piping flowers petal by petal. These piping tips are much larger, and they differ from regular piping tips because instead of a single shaped opening at one end, the tip is a finely designed cutout. There are several cutouts on the end that produce different shapes to collectively form one design. With such an intricately designed tip, one squeeze of the piping bag will produce a complete flower. Unlike other piping tips, there are no numbers on Russian piping tips, so the only way to distinguish them is by the designs on the nozzles. The more detailed the design on the piping tip, the more detailed the buttercream flower will be.

The key to producing beautiful, realistic flowers with Russian piping tips lies in the buttercream's consistency. If the buttercream is too warm or soft, the design might not be as defined. If the buttercream is too cold or firm, the buttercream might break off and not create a clean edge. It is important to pipe a few test flowers with these piping tips to make sure your buttercream is the ideal consistency. In addition to ensuring the correct consistency of the buttercream, tinting the buttercream with more than one color can add depth to each piped flower. In the same piping bag fitted with a Russian piping tip, fill the piping bag with buttercream in two different colors. When piped, the buttercream flower will have some darker petals and some lighter petals.

What you need:

- Buttercream tinted with pink gel food coloring (page 149)
- Buttercream tinted with green gel food coloring (page 149)
- 2 pastry bags
- Russian piping tips of choice
- Wilton #67 tip (for leaves)

Fill a pastry bag fitted with a Russian piping tip of your choice with pink buttercream. Place the tip at a 90-degree angle on the surface of the cupcake or cake. Using moderate pressure, squeeze the bag until the flower builds a base on the cupcake or cake. In a quick burst, pull the bag straight up, releasing the pressure on the pastry bag at the same time. (For cupcakes, start in the center with either one flower or a cluster of three flowers, then pipe the rest of the flowers all around until the cupcake's surface has been covered.)

Fill a pastry bag fitted with a Wilton #67 tip with green buttercream. Pipe leaves around the base of some of the flowers.

HOLIDAY FLORAL COOKIE BOX TUTORIAL

The one activity I look forward to the most during the holidays is making a festive cookie box. I enjoy making a cookie box more than going to see the holiday light displays, sipping on hot chocolate, or opening presents on Christmas Day. I am not going sugarcoat it and tell you that a cookie box is something you can accomplish in one afternoon. I like to divide the cookie baking into one or two days and assemble the cookie box on the second or third day. Alternatively, you can make this a fun activity to do with friends during the holidays. Think of this as a "cookie potluck." Everyone will be in charge of baking one or two different kinds of cookies, and then everyone will be able to leave with their own cookie box at the end of the night.

There is no specific set of instructions on how to assemble a great cookie box, but here are some tips that can take your cookie box to the next level.

Find the Perfect Box

Old metal cookie tins are perfect to recycle to become new cookie boxes—they were made to hold cookies in the first place! Wooden boxes with lids from craft stores and sturdy gift boxes will also do the trick. Sometimes I like to make cookie box dividers from thick cardstock to separate the different types of cookies in my box.

Have a Variety of Colors and Textures

I like having a variety of cookies in my cookie box—cutout cookies, bar cookies, sandwich cookies, you name it. Not only does having a variety of cookies take your cookie box to the next level visually, but it also makes the cookie box more fun to eat. You get different flavors and textures with every cookie.

Stack Your Cookies

To build an impressive cookie box, you want to have plenty of cookies. You will have to stack some of the cookies to fill up the whole box. Stack the sturdier, thicker cookies at the bottom of the box and place the more delicate ones on top.

Add Treats That Are Not Cookies

Add your favorite candies and chocolates for extra fun! I love adding mini candy canes, marshmallows, or festive lollipops to my boxes. Try adding floral caramels from page 135.

These are the cookies I used to fill my cookie box on page 162:

- Floral Almond Wreath Cookies (page 57)

- Pressed Pansy Sugar Cookies (page 62)

- Lavender Caramel and Mocha Thumbprint Cookies (page 66)

- Lavender-Pistachio Linzer Cookies (page 69)

- Rose Petal Shortbread (page 70)

- Plum Blossom "Window" Cookies (page 72)

- Rose Lollipops (page 136)

Acknowlegments

To Rich, for whom a few sentences in the back of a book is hardly enough for me to show my gratitude and love. Thank you for always being the first reader of a new blog post and first 'like' on an Instagram post, for believing in me more than I ever could, for driving me to the store to get blocks of unsalted butter at midnight, and for always bringing home flowers you knew would inspire me to create. You are the biggest inspiration behind Constellation Inspiration and for that I am grateful.

To Mom and Dad, for being the first to instill in me the idea that making food is one of the best ways to show love. Thank you for searching far and wide for the perfect salted egg yolks for my mooncakes, for voting for me every day for the Saveur Blog Awards, for always finding freezer space for my many cakes and cookies, and for creating a home that fosters love and creativity.

To Tessa and Lyndsay, for sitting down with me two years ago to let me know all the details of your own cookbook experiences and for giving me the courage I needed to start this project. Thank you for always being an endless source of inspiration.

To Thalia, for always checking in on me and being there at 2:47am to talk about cake flavors, the magic of cherry blossoms, and the things we need to make when we get together. You are such an amazing friend, and this blogging and book journey would not have been the same without you.

To Kelsey, for the tremendous amount of support and apple slushies from your farm. I am so happy you decided to meet up and bake with a stranger back in 2016 because that started this wonderful friendship. Thank you for always being such a positive light.

To Victor, for being the blog's first photographer before I picked up my first camera and learned what f/1.8 meant. Thank you for all your beautiful work and great friendship.

To all my other friends, for always being great taste testers and for always being so supportive and understanding when I have to cancel last minute on plans during cookbook deadline periods. I owe all of you so many cookies.

To my editor Lauren and copyeditor Nichole, for always reminding me that I need to specify my mixer's speed for making batter, for your patience, and for believing in me and making this project possible.

Most of all, thank you to all the readers of Constellation Inspiration, who decided that out of the many blogs out there, mine was special and decided to follow along on this journey. None of this would have been possible without each and every one of you.

About the Author

Amy is a self-taught baker and blogger from Vancouver, BC, who believes in moments of sweetness, the magic of butter and sugar, and the ability of flowers to make anything and everything more beautiful. Amy started her blog Constellation Inspiration, a buttercream-coated journal full of recipes and love letters dedicated to all things sweet, four years ago while she was in graduate school. Since then, she has created many layer cakes, conquered her fear of making choux pastry, and been nominated for a Saveur Blog Award.

Index

A

All-Butter Pie Crust

   Floral Hand Pies, 103–104

   Peach Galette with Lavender Whipped Cream, 101–102

   Pear Pie with Pressed-Flower Crust, 107–108

   Strawberry-Rose Pie, 97–98

almonds

   Hibiscus-Glazed Apple-Pistachio Frangipane Tart, 115–117

   Strawberry, Rhubarb, and Rose Frangipane Tart, 114

Apple-Rose Custard Tart, 121–122

Apple Roses, 122

apples

   Apple-Rose Custard Tart, 122

   "Flowerfetti" Brown Butter Apple Cake with Cream Cheese Buttercream, 33–34

   Hibiscus-Glazed Apple-Pistachio Frangipane Tart, 117

B

bars

   Mixed Berry-Lavender Streusel Bars, 61

   Rose Petal Shortbread, 70

blackberries

   Mixed Berry-Lavender Streusel Bars, 61

   Summer Fruit Tart, 111

blueberries: Jasmine-Blueberry Ice Cream Choux Puffs, 83–84

buttercream

   Chocolate Buttercream, 22

   Chocolate-Lavender Buttercream, 46

   Cream Cheese Buttercream, 25, 34

   Lemon Buttercream, 21

   Lemon-Elderflower Buttercream, 45

   Mascarpone Buttercream, 18

   Perfect Vanilla Buttercream for Piping, 149

   Rose Mascarpone Buttercream, 42

   Vanilla Buttercream, 16, 29

   Vanilla Swiss Meringue Buttercream, 36

   Whipped Vanilla Buttercream, 49

buttermilk

   Chocolate Bundt Cake with Orange Blossom Ganache, 39

   Elderflower-Strawberry Buttermilk Cake, 21

   White Chocolate Cake with Rose Mascarpone, 40–42

C

cakes

   assembly considerations, 143

   baking considerations, 142

   Chamomile Cake with Peach and Mascarpone Buttercream, 17–18

   Cherry Blossom Almond Layer Cake, 25

   Chocolate Bundt Cake with Orange Blossom Ganache, 39

   Chocolate-Lilac Cake with Chocolate Buttercream, 22

   decorating, 142–143

   Elderflower-Strawberry Buttermilk Cake, 21

   "Flowerfetti" Brown Butter Apple Cake with Cream Cheese Buttercream, 33–34

   Jasmine and Vanilla Bundt Cake, 26

   Lavender Cake with Creamy Lemon Curd and Vanilla Buttercream, 15–16

   One-Bowl Chocolate Sheet Cake with Buttercream Flowers, 29

   Persian Love Cake, 30

   storage considerations, 143

   White Chocolate Cake with Rose Mascarpone, 40–42

Woodland Pear Cake with Chestnut and Vanilla Swiss Meringue Buttercream, 35–36

candies

Candied Petals, 145

Rose Lollipops, 136

caramels: Floral Caramels, 135

chamomile flowers: Chamomile Cake with Peach and Mascarpone Buttercream, 17–18

chamomile tea

Chamomile Cake with Peach and Mascarpone Buttercream, 17–18

Chamomile Whipped Cream, 80

Mango Curd, 80

cherries

Cherry Blossom Almond Layer Cake, 25

Cherry Blossom Sablés, 54

Summer Fruit Tart, 111

Whipped Cherry Blossom Ganache, 77–78

chestnut puree: Woodland Pear Cake with Chestnut and Vanilla Swiss Meringue Buttercream, 35–36

Chewy Lavender–Earl Grey Sugar Cookies, 53

chocolate

Chocolate Bundt Cake with Orange Blossom Ganache, 39

Chocolate Buttercream, 22

Chocolate Ganache, 92

Chocolate-Lavender Buttercream, 46

Chocolate-Lavender Religieuse, 91–92

Chocolate-Lilac Cake with Chocolate Buttercream, 22

Coffee and Milk Chocolate Cream Puffs with Candied Rose Petals, 86

Dark and White Chocolate-Lavender Cookies, 58

Dark Chocolate-Lavender Pastry Cream, 91–92

Lavender Caramel and Mocha Thumbprint Cookies, 66

Lavender "Hot Chocolate" Cupcakes, 46

One-Bowl Chocolate Sheet Cake with Buttercream Flowers, 29

Whipped Milk Chocolate Ganache, 86

chocolate, white

Dark and White Chocolate-Lavender Cookies, 58

Jasmine and Honey Éclairs, 89–90

Jasmine Fruit Tartlets, 124

Lavender-White Chocolate Ganache, 69

Orange Blossom Ganache, 39

Whipped Cherry Blossom Ganache, 77–78

Whipped Jasmine-Green Tea Ganache, 124

White Chocolate Cake with Rose Mascarpone, 40–42

White Chocolate, Pistachio, and Orange Blossom Cookies, 65

choux

Chamomile-Mango Cream Puffs, 79–80

Chocolate-Lavender Religieuse, 91–92

Coffee and Milk Chocolate Cream Puffs with Candied Rose Petals, 85–86

Jasmine and Honey Éclairs, 89–90

Jasmine-Blueberry Ice Cream Choux Puffs, 83–84

Whipped Cherry Blossom Ganache and Matcha Cream Puffs, 77–78

chrysanthemum piping tutorial, 158

coconut milk

Jasmine Mooncakes, 132

Rose Blossom Mochi, 129

coffee

Chocolate-Lilac Cake with Chocolate Buttercream, 22

Coffee and Milk Chocolate Cream Puffs with Candied Rose Petals, 85–86

Coffee Whipped Cream, 86

Lavender Caramel and Mocha Thumbprint Cookies, 66

One-Bowl Chocolate Sheet Cake with Buttercream Flowers, 29

cookies

Cherry Blossom Sablés, 54

Chewy Lavender–Earl Grey Sugar Cookies, 53

Dark and White Chocolate-Lavender Cookies, 58

Floral Almond Wreath Cookies, 57

holiday cookie box, 163

Lavender Caramel and Mocha Thumbprint Cookies, 66

Lavender-Pistachio Linzer Cookies, 69

Mixed Berry-Lavender Streusel Bars, 61

No-Churn Rose-Pistachio Ice Cream Sandwiches, 130

Plum Blossom "Window" Cookies, 72-73

Pressed Pansy Sugar Cookies, 62

Rose Petal Shortbread, 70

White Chocolate, Pistachio, and Orange Blossom Cookies, 65

cream cheese

Cream Cheese Buttercream, 25, 34

Jasmine and Vanilla Bundt Cake, 26

No-Bake Honey Blossom Cheesecake Tart with Plums, 118

Creamy Lemon Curd, 15-16

cupcakes

Lavender "Hot Chocolate" Cupcakes, 46

Lemon-Ricotta Cupcakes with Lemon-Elderflower Buttercream, 43-45

Lilac-Vanilla Cupcakes, 49

currants: Summer Fruit Tart, 111

D

Dark and White Chocolate-Lavender Cookies, 58

decorations

cakes, 142-143

Candied Petals, 145

edible flowers, 140, 146

holiday floral cookie box, 163

inedible flowers, 140

piping, 149-160

Pressed Edible Flowers, 146

E

éclairs: Jasmine and Honey Éclairs, 89-90

eggs

All-Butter Pie Crust, 97-98

Apple-Rose Custard Tart, 121-122

Chamomile Cake with Peach and Mascarpone Buttercream, 17-18

Chamomile-Mango Cream Puffs, 79-80, 80

Cherry Blossom Almond Layer Cake, 25

Chewy Lavender-Earl Grey Sugar Cookies, 53

Chocolate Bundt Cake with Orange Blossom Ganache, 39

Chocolate-Lavender Religieuse, 91-92

Chocolate-Lilac Cake with Chocolate Buttercream, 22

Coffee and Milk Chocolate Cream Puffs with Candied Rose Petals, 85-86

Creamy Lemon Curd, 15-16

Dark and White Chocolate-Lavender Cookies, 58

Dark Chocolate-Lavender Pastry Cream, 91-92

Elderflower-Strawberry Buttermilk Cake, 21

Floral Hand Pies, 103-104

"Flowerfetti" Brown Butter Apple Cake with Cream Cheese Buttercream, 33-34

Hibiscus-Glazed Apple-Pistachio Frangipane Tart, 115-117

Jasmine and Honey Éclairs, 89-90

Jasmine-Blueberry Ice Cream Choux Puffs, 83-84

Jasmine Fruit Tartlets, 124

Jasmine Mooncakes, 132-133

Lavender Cake with Creamy Lemon Curd and Vanilla Buttercream, 15-16

Lavender Caramel and Mocha Thumbprint Cookies, 66

Lavender "Hot Chocolate" Cupcakes, 46

Lavender-Pistachio Linzer Cookies, 69

Lemon-Ricotta Cupcakes with Lemon-Elderflower Buttercream, 43-45

Lilac-Vanilla Cupcakes, 49

One-Bowl Chocolate Sheet Cake with Buttercream Flowers, 29

Peach Galette with Lavender Whipped Cream, 101-102

Pear Pie with Pressed-Flower Crust, 107-108

Persian Love Cake, 30

Pressed Pansy Sugar Cookies, 62

Strawberry, Rhubarb, and Rose Frangipane Tart, 112–114

Summer Fruit Tart, 111

Vanilla Swiss Meringue Buttercream, 36

Whipped Cherry Blossom Ganache and Matcha Cream Puffs, 77–78

White Chocolate Cake with Rose Mascarpone, 40–42

White Chocolate, Pistachio, and Orange Blossom Cookies, 65

Woodland Pear Cake with Chestnut and Vanilla Swiss Meringue Buttercream, 35–36

elderflowers

Elderflower-Strawberry Buttermilk Cake, 21

Lemon-Elderflower Buttercream, 45

Lemon-Ricotta Cupcakes with Lemon-Elderflower Buttercream, 43–45

F

figs: Persian Love Cake, 30

Floral Almond Wreath Cookies, 57

Floral Caramels, 135

Floral Hand Pies, 103–104

"Flowerfetti" Brown Butter Apple Cake with Cream Cheese Buttercream, 33–34

frosting

Chocolate Buttercream, 22

Chocolate-Lavender Buttercream, 46

Cream Cheese Buttercream, 25, 34

Lemon Buttercream, 21

Lemon-Elderflower Buttercream, 45

Mascarpone Buttercream, 18

Perfect Vanilla Buttercream for Piping, 149

Rose Mascarpone Buttercream, 42

Vanilla Buttercream, 16, 29

Vanilla Swiss Meringue Buttercream, 36

Whipped Vanilla Buttercream, 49

G

galettes: Peach Galette with Lavender Whipped Cream, 101–102

ganache

Chocolate Ganache, 92

Lavender-White Chocolate Ganache, 69

Orange Blossom Ganache, 39

Whipped Cherry Blossom Ganache, 77–78

Whipped Jasmine-Green Tea Ganache, 124

Whipped Jasmine-Honey Ganache, 89–90

Whipped Milk Chocolate Ganache, 86

glazes

Hibiscus-Lemon Glaze, 117

Royal Icing Glaze, 57, 86, 104

gold leaf

Chocolate-Lavender Religieuse, 92

Persian Love Cake, 30

Rose Lollipops, 136

Woodland Pear Cake with Chestnut and Vanilla Swiss Meringue Buttercream, 35–36

H

heavy cream

Apple-Rose Custard Tart, 121–122

Chamomile Whipped Cream, 80

Chocolate Ganache, 92

Chocolate-Lavender Religieuse, 91–92

Coffee Whipped Cream, 86

Dark Chocolate-Lavender Pastry Cream, 91–92

Floral Caramels, 135

Jasmine-Blueberry Ice Cream, 83–84

Jasmine Fruit Tartlets, 124

Lavender Caramel and Mocha Thumbprint Cookies, 66

Lavender Whipped Cream, 102

Lavender-White Chocolate Ganache, 69

Matcha Whipped Cream, 78

No-Bake Honey Blossom Cheesecake Tart with Plums, 118

No-Churn Rose-Pistachio Ice Cream Sandwiches, 130

Orange Blossom Ganache, 39

Persian Love Cake, 30

Rose-Mascarpone Whipped Cream, 111

Whipped Cherry Blossom Ganache, 77–78

Whipped Cream, 92

Whipped Jasmine-Green Tea Ganache, 124

Whipped Jasmine-Honey Ganache, 89–90

Whipped Milk Chocolate Ganache, 86

hibiscus

Hibiscus-Glazed Apple-Pistachio Frangipane Tart, 117

Hibiscus-Lemon Glaze, 117

holiday floral cookie box, 163

honey

Jasmine and Honey Éclairs, 89–90

No-Bake Honey Blossom Cheesecake Tart with Plums, 118

Whipped Jasmine-Honey Ganache, 89–90

I

ice cream

Jasmine-Blueberry Ice Cream, 83–84

No-Churn Rose-Pistachio Ice Cream Sandwiches, 130

icing: Royal Icing Glaze, 57, 86, 104

isomalt crystals: Plum Blossom "Window" Cookies, 72–73

J

jam: Mixed Berry-Lavender Streusel Bars, 61

jasmine

Apple-Rose Custard Tart, 121–122

Floral Caramels, 135

Jasmine and Honey Éclairs, 89–90

Jasmine and Vanilla Bundt Cake, 26

Jasmine Fruit Tartlets, 124

Whipped Jasmine-Honey Ganache, 89–90

jasmine green tea

Apple-Rose Custard Tart, 121–122

Jasmine Fruit Tartlets, 124

Whipped Jasmine-Green Tea Ganache, 124

L

lavender

Chewy Lavender-Earl Grey Sugar Cookies, 53

Chocolate-Lavender Buttercream, 46

Chocolate-Lavender Religieuse, 91–92

Dark and White Chocolate-Lavender Cookies, 58

Dark Chocolate-Lavender Pastry Cream, 91–92

Lavender Cake with Creamy Lemon Curd and Vanilla Buttercream, 15–16

Lavender Caramel and Mocha Thumbprint Cookies, 66

Lavender Whipped Cream, 102

Lavender-White Chocolate Ganache, 69

Mixed Berry-Lavender Streusel Bars, 61

lemon juice

Chamomile Cake with Peach and Mascarpone Buttercream, 18

Chamomile-Mango Cream Puffs, 80

Creamy Lemon Curd, 15–16

Hibiscus-Glazed Apple-Pistachio Frangipane Tart, 117

Lavender Cake with Creamy Lemon Curd and Vanilla Buttercream, 15–16

Lemon Buttercream, 21

Lemon-Elderflower Buttercream, 45

Lemon-Ricotta Cupcakes with Lemon-Elderflower Buttercream, 43–45

Mango Curd, 80

Peach Galette with Lavender Whipped Cream, 101–102

Pear Pie with Pressed-Flower Crust, 107–108

Strawberry-Rose Pie, 97–98

lemon zest

Elderflower-Strawberry Buttermilk Cake, 21

Lemon Buttercream, 21

Lemon-Elderflower Buttercream, 45

Lemon-Ricotta Cupcakes with Lemon-Elderflower Buttercream, 43–45

Peach Galette with Lavender Whipped Cream, 101–102

lilac

Chocolate-Lilac Cake with Chocolate Buttercream, 22

Lilac-Vanilla Cupcakes, 49

lollipops: Rose Lollipops, 136

luster dust: Woodland Pear Cake with Chestnut and Vanilla Swiss Meringue Buttercream, 35–36

M

mango
   Chamomile-Mango Cream Puffs, 80
   Mango Curd, 80

marshmallows: Lavender "Hot Chocolate" Cupcakes, 46

mascarpone
   Chamomile Cake with Peach and Mascarpone Buttercream, 18
   Rose Mascarpone Buttercream, 42
   Rose-Mascarpone Whipped Cream, 111
   Summer Fruit Tart, 111

matcha powder: Matcha Whipped Cream, 78

milk, coconut
   Jasmine Mooncakes, 132
   Rose Blossom Mochi, 129

milk, sweetened condensed: No-Churn Rose-Pistachio Ice Cream Sandwiches, 130

milk, whole
   Apple-Rose Custard Tart, 121–122
   Chamomile Cake with Peach and Mascarpone Buttercream, 17–18
   Chamomile-Mango Cream Puffs, 79–80
   Cherry Blossom Almond Layer Cake, 25
   Chocolate Buttercream, 22

Chocolate-Lavender Buttercream, 46

Chocolate-Lavender Religieuse, 91–92

Coffee and Milk Chocolate Cream Puffs with Candied Rose Petals, 85–86

Cream Cheese Buttercream, 25, 34

Dark Chocolate-Lavender Pastry Cream, 91–92

Floral Almond Wreath Cookies, 57

"Flowerfetti" Brown Butter Apple Cake with Cream Cheese Buttercream, 33–34

Jasmine and Honey Éclairs, 89–90

Jasmine-Blueberry Ice Cream Choux Puffs, 83–84, 84

Jasmine Mooncakes, 132

Lavender Cake with Creamy Lemon Curd and Vanilla Buttercream, 15

Lavender "Hot Chocolate" Cupcakes, 46

Lemon Buttercream, 21

Lilac-Vanilla Cupcakes, 49

Perfect Vanilla Buttercream for Piping, 149

Persian Love Cake, 30

Rose Mascarpone Buttercream, 42

Royal Icing Glaze, 86, 104

Strawberry-Rose Pie, 97–98

Vanilla Buttercream, 16, 29

Whipped Cherry Blossom Ganache and Matcha Cream Puffs, 77–78

Whipped Vanilla Buttercream, 49

Woodland Pear Cake with Chestnut and Vanilla Swiss Meringue Buttercream, 35–36

Mixed Berry-Lavender Streusel Bars, 61

mochi: Rose Blossom Mochi, 129

mooncakes: Jasmine Mooncakes, 132–133

N

No-Bake Honey Blossom Cheesecake Tart with Plums, 118

O

oats: Mixed Berry-Lavender Streusel Bars, 61

One-Bowl Chocolate Sheet Cake with Buttercream Flowers, 29

orange blossom
   No-Bake Honey Blossom Cheesecake Tart with Plums, 118
   Orange Blossom Ganache, 39
   White Chocolate, Pistachio, and Orange Blossom Cookies, 65

orange juice
   Apple-Rose Custard Tart, 122
   Floral Hand Pies, 103–104

orange zest: Persian Love Cake, 30

P

pansies: Pressed Pansy Sugar Cookies, 62

peaches
  Chamomile Cake with Peach and
    Mascarpone Buttercream, 18
  Peach Galette with Lavender
    Whipped Cream, 101–102

pears
  Pear Pie with Pressed-Flower Crust,
    107–108
  Woodland Pear Cake with Chestnut
    and Vanilla Swiss Meringue
    Buttercream, 35–36
  Perfect Vanilla Buttercream for Piping,
    149
  Persian Love Cake, 30

pies
  Floral Hand Pies, 103–104
  Peach Galette with Lavender
    Whipped Cream, 101–102
  Pear Pie with Pressed-Flower Crust,
    107–108
  Strawberry-Rose Pie, 97–98

piping
  buttercream consistency, 149
  chrysanthemum tutorial, 158
  Perfect Vanilla Buttercream for
    Piping, 149
  ranunculus tutorial, 153
  rose tutorial, 150
  ruffled peony tutorial, 154
  Russian tips, 160
  sunflower tutorial, 157

pistachios
  Lavender-Pistachio Linzer Cookies,
    69

Hibiscus-Glazed Apple-Pistachio
    Frangipane Tart, 115–117
No-Churn Rose-Pistachio Ice Cream
    Sandwiches, 130
Persian Love Cake, 30
White Chocolate, Pistachio, and
    Orange Blossom Cookies, 65

plums
  No-Bake Honey Blossom
    Cheesecake Tart with Plums,
    118
  Plum Blossom "Window" Cookies,
    72–73

Pressed Pansy Sugar Cookies, 62

R

ranunculus piping tutorial, 153
raspberries: No-Churn Rose-Pistachio
    Ice Cream Sandwiches, 130
rhubarb
  Roasted Rhubarb, 114
  Strawberry, Rhubarb, and Rose
    Compote, 112–114
  Strawberry, Rhubarb, and Rose
    Frangipane Tart, 112–114, 114
ricotta cheese: Lemon-Ricotta
    Cupcakes with Lemon-
    Elderflower Buttercream,
    43–45
Roasted Rhubarb, 114
roses
  Coffee and Milk Chocolate Cream
    Puffs with Candied Rose Petals,
    86
  Persian Love Cake, 30
  piping tutorial, 150

Rose Lollipops, 136
Rose Petal Shortbread, 70
White Chocolate Cake with Rose
    Mascarpone, 40–42

rose water
  No-Churn Rose-Pistachio Ice Cream
    Sandwiches, 130
  Persian Love Cake, 30
  Rose Blossom Mochi, 129
  Rose Lollipops, 136
  Rose Mascarpone Buttercream, 42
  Rose-Mascarpone Whipped Cream,
    111
  Royal Icing Glaze, 57, 86
  Strawberry, Rhubarb, and Rose
    Frangipane Tart, 112–114
  Strawberry-Rose Pie, 97–98
Royal Icing Glaze, 104
Russian piping tips, 160

S

sour cream
  Chamomile Cake with Peach and
    Mascarpone Buttercream,
    17–18
  Cherry Blossom Almond Layer
    Cake, 25
  Chocolate Bundt Cake with Orange
    Blossom Ganache, 39
  Jasmine and Vanilla Bundt Cake, 26
  Lavender Cake with Creamy
    Lemon Curd and Vanilla
    Buttercream, 15–16
  Lavender "Hot Chocolate" Cupcakes,
    46

Lilac-Vanilla Cupcakes, 49

Woodland Pear Cake with Chestnut and Vanilla Swiss Meringue Buttercream, 35–36

strawberries

Elderflower-Strawberry Buttermilk Cake, 21

Floral Hand Pies, 103–104

Lemon-Ricotta Cupcakes with Lemon-Elderflower Buttercream, 43–45

Mixed Berry-Lavender Streusel Bars, 61

Strawberry, Rhubarb, and Rose Frangipane Tart, 112–114

Strawberry-Rose Pie, 97–98

Summer Fruit Tart, 111

Summer Fruit Tart, 111

sunflower piping tutorial, 157

sweetened condensed milk: No-Churn Rose-Pistachio Ice Cream Sandwiches, 130

T

tarts

Apple-Rose Custard Tart, 121–122

Hibiscus-Glazed Apple-Pistachio Frangipane Tart, 115–117

Jasmine Fruit Tartlets, 124

No-Bake Honey Blossom Cheesecake Tart with Plums, 118

Strawberry, Rhubarb, and Rose Frangipane Tart, 112–114

Summer Fruit Tart, 111

tea

Apple-Rose Custard Tart, 121–122

Chamomile Cake with Peach and Mascarpone Buttercream, 17–18

Chamomile Whipped Cream, 80

Chewy Lavender-Earl Grey Sugar Cookies, 53

Jasmine Fruit Tartlets, 124

Whipped Jasmine-Green Tea Ganache, 124

V

Vanilla Buttercream, 16, 29

Vanilla Custard, 121–122

Vanilla Swiss Meringue Buttercream, 36

W

Whipped Cherry Blossom Ganache, 77–78

Whipped Cherry Blossom Ganache and Matcha Cream Puffs, 77–78

whipped cream

Chamomile Whipped Cream, 80

Coffee Whipped Cream, 86

Lavender Whipped Cream, 102

Matcha Whipped Cream, 78

Rose-Mascarpone Whipped Cream, 111

Whipped Cream, 92

Whipped Jasmine-Green Tea Ganache, 124

Whipped Jasmine-Honey Ganache, 89

Whipped Milk Chocolate Ganache, 86

Whipped Vanilla Buttercream, 49

White Chocolate Cake with Rose Mascarpone, 40–42

White Chocolate, Pistachio, and Orange Blossom Cookies, 65

Woodland Pear Cake with Chestnut and Vanilla Swiss Meringue Buttercream, 35–36

white chocolate

Dark and White Chocolate-Lavender Cookies, 58

Jasmine and Honey Éclairs, 89–90

Jasmine Fruit Tartlets, 124

Lavender-White Chocolate Ganache, 69

Orange Blossom Ganache, 39

Whipped Cherry Blossom Ganache, 77–78

Whipped Jasmine-Green Tea Ganache, 124

White Chocolate Cake with Rose Mascarpone, 40–42

White Chocolate, Pistachio, and Orange Blossom Cookies, 65

Y

yogurt: "Flowerfetti" Brown Butter Apple Cake with Cream Cheese Buttercream, 33–34